DATE DUE	
FEB 11 1996	MAY - 4 2005
NOV 13 1998	
MAR 14 2001	
MAR - 8 2000	
OCT 16 2001	
AUG 19 2003 SEP 11 2003	

DEMCO, INC. 38-2971

D1212986

JAPAN—A HISTORY IN ART

美と日本人の歴史

JAPAN

A HISTORY IN ART

by Bradley Smith / Spring Books, London · New York · Sydney · Toronto

CONSULTANTS   *Madoka Kanai, University of Tokyo*

Shinichi Nagai, Women's Art University of Tokyo

Kazuko Yamakawa, Bungei Shunju

PHOTOGRAPHY   *Bradley Smith*

ART DIRECTION   *Curtis Fields*

CALLIGRAPHY   *Baikei (Tadashi) Suzuki*

COORDINATOR   *Daniel Stampler*

Published as a Gemini Smith book in the U.S.A.
This edition published 1972 by
The Hamlyn Publishing Group Limited
London · New York · Sydney · Toronto
Hamlyn House, Feltham, Middlesex, England
by arrangement with Gemini Smith, Inc., New York

ISBN   0 600 35225 0

PREFACE

This visual history of Japan is the combined effort of a group of distinguished scholars in the Japanese and western world. The intention is to penetrate the cultural past of this most progressive of Asian countries. It is a sketchbook of history drawn and painted by sensitive artists who worked within one hundred years of the actual events. It is not intended as a definitive political or cultural history, although it contains pertinent elements of both. The goal is to give the reader a visual knowledge of Japan's evolution from prehistoric times to her emergence, at the close of 1912, as a modern world power.

To create such a book, the author has drawn upon the great body of work produced by the artists of Japan over a two thousand year period. He was fortunate in having the cooperation of the large museums, Buddhist temples and Shintō shrines of Japan, and access to the important collections of The Boston Museum of Fine Arts and The Freer Gallery of Washington as well as many private, rarely seen collections.

Because this is a visual treatment of the history of the islands of Japan, there inevitably emerges a history of Japanese art. By linking the two, it is possible to show life as it was lived, historic events as they were recorded, and art as it reflected events great and small in ten periods from Archaic through Meiji.

The writer has had the privilege of consultation with The Honorable Edwin O. Reischauer, historian and United States Ambassador to Japan; Yukio Yashiro, distinguished art historian and critic; Nagatake Asano, Director, Tokyo National Museum; Madoka Kanai, of the University of Tokyo; Shinichi Nagai, of the Women's Art University of Tokyo; and Douglas Overton of the Japan Society.

The works of art are printed in color from new and original photographs to reproduce them as closely as possible to the originals. The reproductions include sculpture from the early periods, when there was little painting to later emphasized screens, scrolls, fans, wall paintings and murals. Color has been used throughout the book because color is an essential part of the visualization given to the people and events by the masters of brush and pen who recorded them.

The canvas of history, as interpreted by the eye and hand of the artist, shows more accurately than words the continuing pageant of drama, comedy, tragedy, despair and joy as the Japanese people sought out their destiny. Because many pictures were taken from rare and fragile scrolls and priceless screens never available to the public, it is possible for the reader to view and enjoy works of art hitherto seen only by the scholar or collector. Here, too, in one volume, are many of the styles, techniques and insights of forty successive generations of artists.

Every effort has been made to make the book objective; to let the events and the illustrations speak for themselves. It is not intended as a work of interpretation, but rather a book of events.

Throughout the book, historical Japanese names have been used in the traditional manner with the family name first.

Because the word "ji," as in Hōryūji, means temple in Japanese, the word temple has not been repeated to identify these famous Buddhist places of worship.

In the chronologies certain liberties have been taken with their traditional structure in the interests of brevity and clarity.

The text is based, so far as possible, upon chronicles of the times but later discoveries in the field of anthropology and history have been considered in this brief outline of Japanese history. In the early chapters the legends of the islands have been retold and labeled as mythology, but this does not mean that, because they are legends, they are without basis in fact.

ACKNOWLEDGEMENTS

A book is never created without the assistance of many people. *JAPAN—A HISTORY IN ART* is no exception, and the author wishes to gratefully acknowledge the help of Japanese and Western experts in their respective fields.

The cooperating museums, temples and shrines in Japan were: Tokyo National Museum, Kobe Municipal Museum, Atami Art Museum, Museum of Modern Art of Tokyo, Hibiya Library, Local History Archives of Tokyo, Mitsui Collection Museum of Kokugakuin University, Tokyo University Historiographical Collection, Kyoto National Museum, Okura Shūkokan Museum, Yamato Bunka Kan Museum, Suntory Gallery, Chūgūji, Daitokuji, Hōryūji, Jingoji, Jōbonrendaiji, Kōdaiji, Kōfukuji, Kōryūji, Reihōkan of Kōyasan, Shōjōji, Tōdaiji, Yakushiji, Kitanojinja, Sudahachiman, and the Imperial Household Agency. In the United States: The Museum of Fine Arts of Boston, The Freer Gallery of Art of the Smithsonian Institution of Washington D. C.

I am grateful to the following private collectors who gave generously of their time and who graciously allowed me to reproduce important examples from their collections: Mr. Tsuneo Tamba of Yokohama, Mr. Paul C. Blum, Mr. Carl H. Boehringer, Mr. C. H. Mitchell, Mr. Raymond Bushell, Mr. Takakiyo Mitsui, Mr. Masasuke Kusumoto, Mr. Takeo Nakazawa, Mr. Hachiro Ohashi, Mrs. Kane Yamazaki and Mr. Nagamichi Kuroda of Tokyo, and Mr. Harold P. Stern of Washington, D. C.

I appreciate the advice and arrangements made by the following members of the personnel of various museums, temples and shrines which I visited: Reverend Shinkai Hotta of Reihōkan Museum, Reverend Kengaku Taniuchi of Jingoji. Mr. Tsuneo Endoh of the Yamato Bunka Kan Museum, Mr. Takeshi Endo of the Local History Archives, Mr. Eizo Yamaguchi of the Mitsui Collection, Mr. Kiyoyuki Higuchi of Kokugakuin University, Mr. Eizo Okura of Okura Museum, Mr. Jiro Umezu of Kyoto National Museum, Mr. Chikashige Arao of Kobe Municipal Museum, Mr. Shigetaka Kaneko of the Tokyo National Museum, Mr. Robert Paine and Miss Emily Biederman of The Museum of Fine Arts in Boston. I am grateful to Mr. Kenjiro Sumimoto and to Mr. Yukio Yashiro of the National Committee for the Protection of Cultural Properties who arranged permission for me to photograph certain national treasures.

I am deeply indebted to the following individuals for their assistance in making arrangements for me to secure photographs of many of the works shown in these pages: Mr. Akira Sono, Director of the Public Information and Cultural Affairs Bureau, Mr. Toshiro Shimanouchi, Mr. Tsutomu Wada, Mr. Keiichi Tachibana, Mr. Kuniaki Asomura and Mr. Alan D. Smith; all of the Ministry of Foreign Affairs in Japan (Gaimusho), Mrs. Kazuko Yamakawa of Bungei Shunju, Dr. Paul Langer of Santa Monica, California, Mr. Douglas Overton of the Japan Society of the United States.

For editorial consultation and assistance, I wish to thank, first, my old friend Sidney Hertzberg of New York City, who assisted in editing the manuscript. I am also grateful to Mr. H. Carroll Parrish and Mr. Koichi Kawana of the University of California at Los Angeles, Mr. Andrew Crichton, Mr. Al Cullison and Miss Sharon Smith. I am especially grateful to The Honorable Edwin O. Reischauer, United States Ambassador to Japan, who read and commented informally upon the final text.

Special thanks to Mr. Shinpei Ikejima of Bungei Shunju who offered help in many areas and who showed his confidence in this book by becoming publisher of it in the Japanese language. Credit also goes to Mr. Iwajiro Noda and Mr. Ty Shigematsu of the famous Okura Hotel in Tokyo and Benrido Photographic Company of Kyoto.

Thanks are due to my devoted secretaries, Mrs. Florence Kronfeld of Escondido, California, Miss Joan Lewis of New York City, and Mrs. Ruth M. Katsurayama of Tokyo.

Finally, my thanks to my wife, Ruth, whose patience, good humor, and assistance helped to make my research, photography and writing a pleasant and rewarding experience.

INTRODUCTION TO THE HISTORY OF JAPAN

by Marius B. Jansen

Professor of History, Princeton University

The story of the Japanese people is of compelling interest for the light it throws on the position and culture of one of the world's strikingly individual societies. It is a history of an island people both master of and mastered by its environment, a people responsive to the setting in which it developed and yet not content to accept its limitations.

The response of the Japanese to their environment has taken many forms. The islands of Japan with their rugged coasts, fertile valleys and mountainous interior have a beauty of form and color that speaks to visitor and native alike. The Japanese have lived close to an ever-changing nature, their patterns of life and forms of architecture alike calculated to make them sensitive to the moods and the sovereignty of season and storm. No literature makes closer and more regular use of season and of sentiment than that of Japan, and no poetry presumes so intimate an appreciation of the hues, sounds and forms of plant, insect and bird.

This spontaneous response to nature and beauty found an early and enduring focus in the cult of Shintō, with whose gods the Japanese first peopled their island home. Conceived as a relatively simple expression of awe and gratitude before the forces of nature, Shintō ritual invoked the spirits helpful to agricultural pursuits. The Sun Goddess was the highest of a myriad of deities who had brought forth the divine land of Japan. Since she was the progenitress of the Imperial clan, her cult associated religion with government and provided an important point of continuity throughout Japanese history. Shintō taught little of morality or worship, and its gods were approached and propitiated by ceremonial purification and ablution. The cult was essentially the work of an agricultural people who saw in natural settings and phenomena the condition of their survival. The association of religion with cleanliness, the seasonal communal festivals, the expression of collective joy and gratitude, the mobilization for this purpose of village youths in boisterous display of energy and strength as the procession carrying the shrine snaked its way through narrow lanes and streets—all were aspects of the joyous and uncomplicated response to nature that the Japanese made through Shintō. Occasionally submerged by the more complex stream of religious and philosophical thought that flowed into Japan from China, Shintō never completely lost its hold on rural Japan. In modern times its expressions have ranged from the state cult of Emperor-centered nationalism to the student celebration-demonstration with its echoes of a simpler rural past.

There is also a significant relationship between other aspects of the Japanese attitude and this setting of emotion and of nature. The literary form most prized by the Japanese has been the short poem: a tantalizingly brief setting using seasonal imagery for its associative burden of emotion, capped by a quick flash of experience expressing pain, melancholy or joy. Bound by rigid conventions, this combination of discipline and intuitive evocation may serve as the literary expression of the illumination so often sought in the discipline of Japanese Buddhism. Again, the flash of inspiration after arduous preparation, the expression of freedom under convention and discipline, is equally characteristic of numerous Japanese sports. In judo, sumō and fencing, as in other contexts, it is the sudden stroke of timing and of insight that governs the outcome. It would be an exaggeration to link all of this to environment in a rigid manner, but taken together, these expressions of preference for the emotive, associative and intuitive may represent extensions of that closeness to nature and the emotions it conveys that have been so often noted by students of Japanese civilization.

Japan's insularity has had important consequences in her relations with the outside world. For the Japanese, China was Greece and Rome: the source of their writing system, of their classics of philosophy, ethics and history, and their transmitter of Buddhism. And since China, unlike the Mediterranean classical world, remained creative and puissant, fresh inspiration and ideas continued to enter Japan. Inevitably Japanese writers, artists and leaders became and remained conscious of the colossus on the mainland, responding with affection or with fear, enthusiasm or reluctance, to the mighty political presence and cultural example. They could neither forget nor ignore it.

But the distance from Japan to China was far greater than that which separated Britain and France, and the contact between the neighbors was of a special kind. Though intense during periods of peak cultural influence, it was necessarily limited and directed rather than general and spontaneous. It represented more a Japanese desire to reach out than a Chinese desire to conquer, and, with the single exception of invasion by the non-Chinese Mongol Emperors, any Japanese decision to reduce the contact went unchallenged by China.

Outside influence and the importation of new modes of thought came therefore in waves rather than in a continuous flow, and coincided with a readiness for new patterns in Japan. The first period of Chinese influence came when Japanese leaders were groping for patterns of legitimacy and organization in order to replace the clan structure with a formal governmental system; the second when that system in turn was giving way to feudalism; and a third when feudalism was taking on new patterns of bureaucratic order and rationality. It was thus the T'ang, Sung and Ming dynasties whose patterns of thought most influenced Japan.

These transfusions from China, directed and purposive as they were in Japanese application, were followed by periods of adaptation and modification. As a result Japanese "borrowing" was seldom imitation, and throughout the whole process the Japanese never, in Sir George Sansom's words, surrendered the inmost stronghold of their own tradition. This became indeed a constant in the Japanese experience, equally true of later influence from the West. Whether introduced under Shōtoku or Meiji, revolutionary innovations that might have been expected to leave Japan unrecognizable have, after a time, been so assimilated as to leave no doubt of the continuity of the native tradition and of the toughness of those qualities in Japan that resist change. Thus, the poetic tradition has gone forward almost without a break; those trends within Confucian thought that are congenial to Japanese ideals of loyalty and sacrifice are the ones which have most developed; and those aspects of Buddhism most akin to Japanese esthetic and emotive proclivities—from popular faith revivals to the non-scriptural illumination of Zen—are the ones that have taken firmest root. No institution imported from China ever obscured the hierarchy of clans at the Heian court. Certainly, Japan was altered by its contacts with China and later with the West. Confucian ethics, Buddhist *karma* and compassion, and later technological and political changes did make deep and permanent imprint. Yet the Japanese tradition has never been submerged, and it reappears in ever fresh and vital form.

Inevitably, this consciousness of the outside world served to heighten awareness of the world within. Self-awareness and identity, a recurrent concern in Japanese philosophy, had its political parallel in the early sense of distinctiveness. The myth of the Sun Goddess and of the Imperial descent, the awareness of China's far more turbulent political course of dynastic upheaval, the successful repulse of the Mongol invasion, and the careful cultivation of distinctive feudal realms all contributed to this process.

Trends toward nationalism put down particularly strong roots in Japan during the Tokugawa period, but they were growing long before that. Of particular importance is the strength of the warrior tradition. The *haniwa* figures of the clan period provide evidence of a warrior spirit and tradition at the dawn of Japanese history, and the Shintō mythology recounts the forcible unification of Japan by the Imperial clan. Military values seemed temporarily submerged in Nara and Heian times, but they reappeared in new strength with the rise of great military houses that led to the Kamakura military system. During the political disorder of later centuries a class of military specialists became even more important, and when peace returned to the land with the Tokugawa hegemony, Japan was under the rule of the samurai, now set apart as the highest of the four classes. In the nineteenth-century modernization program, the young samurai reformers utilized education and conscription to popularize and universalize the old samurai code as the center of the value structure of all Japanese.

A major element in the samurai code was the supremacy of political over personal considerations. Always implicit in the organization and requirements of the agricultural community, this obligation now stressed the samurai's duty to his overlord, in whose service he was trained to face death daily. Confucianism, in Imperial China the code of civilian bureaucrats, in Japan laid stress on loyalty and duty. The samurai's loyalty to his lord was paralleled by the duty men owed to masters in other walks of life. The teacher, the landlord, the modern labor boss or political faction head, expected and usually received the loyalty of his subordinates.

In Tokugawa times the policy of national seclusion served to reinforce a sense of cultural distinctiveness. There were also regional seclusion policies practiced by many of the feudal lords, whose paternalistic policies emphasized the importance of building wealth and strength. Despite the feudal decentralization, a solid basis for nationalism developed, and it required only the appearance of a pronounced threat from without, as represented by the intrusive West, to effect a submerging in the national interest of the regional rivalries that seemed unimportant in the face of the larger challenge.

Priority of political over family obligations was never carried so far as to permit denial of family bonds, for this would have been out of harmony with the deepest urgings of the Japanese outlook. Indeed, political and status relationships were often expressed in familial or kinship terms. The feudal vassal, the student, disciple, tenant and laborer referred to his superior in parental terms. Occasionally this terminology became fact, as the lord, teacher, painter or actor accepted his underling into his family line by adoption. The "dynasties" of actors, painters and print-makers thus resembled those of rulers, and bonds of fidelity were strengthened by claims of filiality. Kinship groups like the Tokugawa "clans" were in reality bureaucratic organizations, and similar ties of obligation persisted in many areas of modern Japanese society. The Meiji reformers, in fact, thought of their country as a "family-state," in which family hierarchies were crowned by the father-Emperor in whom all loyalties found focus and expression.

There is also the pattern of indirect rule. Although hierarchy was respected and observed in Imperial and lesser clans, it could not always be assumed that competence was concentrated at the top. The very pinnacle of hierarchy, the Emperor, was too high and austere to concern himself with practical workings of government, and he was speedily surrounded by assistants who restricted his role to ritual. The Fujiwara, who first filled this role, were replaced in time by the heads of the great military houses of Taira, Minamoto, Ashikaga and Tokugawa. At each point, of course, the Emperor's legitimation and sanction was an important element in their prestige and power. Within those houses in turn a similar process was at work, and by the time of Tokugawa Japan, the Shōgun and the feudal lords were frequently little more than symbols of the authority exerted by their inferiors. Because of this diffusion of power and the changes in family lines through adoption, opportunity and responsibility were far more widely shared than the apparently austere lines of control would indicate. Throughout Japanese history the aspect and the actuality of responsibility have often been quite separate.

The history of Japan records a steady increase in the diffusion of culture. For some centuries after the first wave of Chinese influence, knowledge of Buddhism and of Confucianism was narrowly concentrated within the ranks of the court nobility. Institutions of centralization spread this knowledge further, and when power at the center declined, attractions in the provinces began to develop. Buddhism became a simple faith for the masses. In Momoyama and Tokugawa Japan, the multiplication of castle towns and the development of great urban centers at Osaka and Edo signaled the development of a society of great complexity and variety. Provincial feudal lords concerned themselves increasingly with literacy, agronomy and exports to other parts of Japan. Distance between classes was great, but hostility was not widespread. Moralists developed the idea that *bushidō*, the way of the warrior, was not necessarily more important than the "way" of farmers and tradesmen, and thereby contributed to the dignity and earnestness with which the latter approached their tasks. In short, Japan was in many ways very little "behind" the Western world in respect to education, nationalism and bureaucratic complexity of government by the time of the nineteenth century.

It required only a centralizing effort to make uniform and universally available advantages that were already widespread.

The influence of the West with its message of progress and industrialization in the middle of the nineteenth century served as a catalyst. There was no automatic or easy transition to modern ways, but the pace was a rapid one. Once again a Japan whose institutions were in need of revamping reached abroad for ideas: the Meiji Emperor's announcement that wisdom would be sought throughout the world set the blueprint for the first half of his reign. Under slogans like "Rich Country, Strong Army" and "Civilization and Enlightenment," the old and the new were used in dynamic combination. The Emperor was returned to formal authority and his place strengthened by a revived Shintō. National power and welfare were given overwhelming priority over individual goals, and politicians, businessmen and even writers urged efforts "for the good of the country" to bring Japan abreast of international standards.

By the time of the Emperor's death in 1912, their efforts had been crowned with success. Japan had become the first country outside the Western world to industrialize and modernize. Constitutional reforms, diplomatic equality, military victories and territorial acquisitions in Formosa, Manchuria and Korea had established Japan as a great power. Yet, in some minds, the memory of feudalism still lingered. The Emperor's death produced a powerful evocation of the feudal past: General Nogi, captor of Port Arthur, committed suicide, partly to atone for a dishonor he had incurred in the Satsuma Rebellion a third of a century earlier, but mainly to call the nation back to its sense of duty.

Japan's history, then, contains great contrasts between unification and disunity, receptivity and seclusion; it details sweeping changes accompanied by remarkable continuities of spirit and organization; and its themes are as individual and striking, as full of life and color, at once unique and universal, as is the artistic record which follows these pages.

No part of the Japanese story is of greater intrinsic value and no part of it speaks more immediately to our imagination than the work of Japanese artists. Mr. Smith's skillful arrangement of the visual record of Japanese history, much of which he presents for the first time in its original color, allows an extraordinary opportunity to see the history and the leaders of Japan as Japanese artists recorded them. He has neglected neither the warriors nor the workers, the court nor the countinghouse; neither the cultivation of honor nor that of rice; neither the world of the Buddha nor the fleeting pleasures against which he came to warn. This work makes it possible to enter into the world of sensitive observers, almost to participate in the pageant of Japanese history.

—MARIUS B. JANSEN

INTRODUCTION TO THE ART OF JAPAN

by Nagatake Asano

Director, Tokyo National Museum

Because I am Japanese, the art of my country has never seemed to me a thing apart, but rather an integral part of my entire life. I do not know whether this feeling is peculiar to the Japanese, but it seems to me that from the earliest times in our history up to the present, the interplay of sculpture, painting, print-making, indeed the very quality of creativeness that has made these arts important, has been basic to our daily existence. Art is apparent in almost every aspect of Japanese life. The sensitive arrangement of flowers seen in every home, the designs on clothing, varying at different seasons of the year, the hanging scroll paintings found in even the most modest houses and apartments, even our historical celebrations which take the form of colorful spectacles—all bespeak our preoccupation with the arts. In sum, there is no distinct separation of art from life in Japanese tradition. There is only life, and the art of Japan cannot be extracted from it.

As Director of the Tokyo National Museum, I live very close to the art of Japan—so close that I find it difficult to write an introduction to what has always been and still is my environment. For this reason, I am not sure that I can adequately introduce the art of Japan to readers in other countries. But because I believe this to be an original and important book which shows many creative forms and techniques, I shall try to set down my thoughts about various art forms and to explain how these forms were cultivated and how they fitted into our social evolution. In doing so, on the assumption that this is not a book restricted to critics, scholars, and students of art history, but rather a book that has been created for everyone with an interest in my country, it is to the general reader rather than to the specialist that I address myself.

In ancient Japan there was no division between the natural wonders of the earth and the objects made by man. The sound of the wind in the trees was a kind of music that man with his primitive flute soon re-created. The grandeur of the rocks, the ever-changing forms of the sea's waves, the sharply etched outlines of trees against the sky and the overpowering beauty of our mountains— all of these manifestations of nature were part of our artistic heritage. Whether a man carved upon a stone or simply observed the beauty of a stone made no difference. Both had a special quality; both were looked upon with reverence and respect and accepted as part of the living world.

Archeologists and anthropologists have not always agreed about our prehistoric culture, but we have discovered a considerable number of prehistoric objects that throw some light upon the creative instinct as it existed in the ancestors of the Japanese people some 3,000 years ago. In those ancient days, there were no objects that could be called, according to strict modern interpretation, works of art; vessels in the shapes of jars and bowls were created for *use*. Yet it is important for us to note that some of the finds in the most ancient tombs include utilitarian objects with simple decorative patterns added as accessories.

As the generations passed, arbitrary divisions in status began to appear. Social and political evolution created aristocratic limitations. A distinctive culture, at first limited to the leaders of the country and their courts, came into being and, as it developed, was nurtured by the influx of other cultures from outside the Japanese islands. These rich influences from India, Korea and, in particular, China caused great changes and gave impetus to the forward movement of Japanese art. A process of adaptation began which gave a Japanese aspect to many of the borrowed forms, both in sculpture and in painting.

It was in the Asuka period that the foundations of Buddhist art came into being, for in the mid-sixth century the great force of Buddhism that had spread from India to China reached

Japan through Korea. Prince Shōtoku founded Hōryūji, which became the first seat of Buddhist art in Japan. With the continued importation of Sui-T'ang culture from China, Buddhist arts thrived. More temples were erected, and a new kind of artistic endeavor was born as disciples tried to express spiritual concepts in objective form. Statues and paintings of extraordinary beauty were the result of this striving by artists to create objects for man to worship. To the spiritual quality that is found in the Buddhas of the Hakuho era (latter part of the Asuka period), later generations of artists added emotional and intellectual shadings.

When Nara became the center of Japanese government—capital of the budding nation—it became, as well, the center of the arts. To a degree, the arts were coordinated by the state. Religion and religious art dominated the life of the court. As the country prospered, more temples, including the great Tōdaiji, were built. Many of the objects of art now in the Shōsōin (a repository of early Japanese art treasures), belong to this culture, known as Tempyō.

The Heian period, during which the capital moved to Kyoto, saw a new cultural flowering as the emerging great families became both patrons and practitioners of the arts. The supreme objective became the rendering of "depth": the artist tried to express something beyond nature and beyond man's response to nature. It has seemed to me that an almost supernatural effect of darkness pervades the art of those days, but by the middle of the Heian period the "depth and darkness" gradually disappeared, and in sculpture and painting a flat brightness became the quality most sought after.

By this time (the end of the twelfth century) the Chinese influence, especially noticeable in Buddhist paintings, had been well integrated, and a Japanese style began to appear. The twenty-five Bosatsu paintings at Kōyasan and the Fugen Bosatsu painting at the Tokyo National Museum are excellent examples. They have the elegance and brightness typical of their time. The idea of Paradise was introduced by the Buddhist priests Honen and Shinran, and Japanese artists expressed the joy to be found in the world to come. At this time an important art form, the picture hand scroll, first came into being, and painters developed a new style called *yamato-e*. *Yamato-e* means Japanese painting, and these early scrolls with their scenes of everyday life were an expression of a new and distinctive feeling in Japanese art. This type of painting, vividly illustrating both the life of the court and of the countryside, continued and became an important part of the art of the Kamakura period.

With the coming to power of the military, art tended to become more realistic, more subjective. Many a scroll recounted in detail the story of a warrior or a priest. The new military ruling class, seeking an ethic by which warriors could live, found its philosophy in the theory and practice of Zen, a cult based upon a realistic approach to life's problems but dependent on instinct for their solution. In this period an art form called *nisee*, the name given to realistic portrait painting, became popular. The portraits of Taira Shigemori and Minamoto Yoritomo, reproduced in this book, are perhaps the greatest examples of this art form. Sculpture, too, was powerful and realistic.

It was natural that in this period of rising militarism, sword-making should develop into a great art. Fine swords had been made and used for generations, but in Kamakura and Muromachi the individuality and skill of certain sword-makers were outstanding. This skill transcended craftsmanship, and the blades, guards and decorations were appreciated as creative works of art.

In the Muromachi and Momoyama periods, the theory and practice of Zen had enormous influence on the arts. *Sumi-e* (black-and-white ink drawings), introduced from China by Zen priests, were popular and were soon adapted to Japanese technique and subject matter, but the artistic point of view that began with the meditative process remained. *Sumi-e* is a subjective style, projected from deep within the individual. It is instinctive painting that moves forward with no planning or repainting.

In architecture, simplicity and awareness of natural surroundings prevailed through the sixteenth century. Artists seemed to be expressing a desire to move away from the world of human complexities into the simpler world of nature.

Two other great influences were noticeable in the Muromachi period: landscape gardening and the tea ceremony (*cha-no-yu*) became part of the

Japanese artistic tradition. The original meaning of the tea ceremony was to look quietly into oneself and to appreciate nature while meditating within a rustic teahouse.

It was also during this period that Western art, introduced by Jesuit and Franciscan missionaries, was first seen by the Japanese people. The effect of the Westerners on Japan was reflected in the painting of both the late Muromachi and the early Azuchi-Momoyama periods. During Momoyama, castles were decorated in styles that sometimes combined Eastern and Western motifs. In painting, a combination of both Chinese and Japanese techniques resulted in the development of the Kano school. The European influence was also reflected in *namban* screen paintings showing the first Westerners in Japan, the early Portuguese traders.

With the Edo period a new unity came to Japan: the efforts begun by Oda Nobunaga and Toyotomi Hideyoshi to consolidate the country were concluded by Tokugawa Ieyasu. Under his rigid but benevolent rule great strides were made in education, the arts and science; and as education reached more and more people, the arts spread widely among the ordinary folk throughout our islands. By the mid-Edo period the wood-block print called *ukiyo-e* had been introduced, and the artists of this popular medium had created an art of the people that was to reach into every part of the country.

Ukiyo-e was followed by *nishiki-e,* also an art of the people. Wood blocks were used as in *ukiyo-e* but more colors were added. It became possible to print pictures in vivid colors at a low cost. Events, great and small, were depicted in this popular art.

With the Meiji era there came a complete change in the social structure of Japan. Though European and American culture continued to come to our islands, the firm foundations upon which Japanese art had been based were not shaken. We had to seek out our own way, which included learning from the West and adapting the knowledge to our needs.

I have briefly, and I am afraid inadequately, tried to describe some of the peaks reached by Japanese artists in our past. But to me, art has no past or present. The Buddhist art of the Nara period, the darkness and the brightness of the Heian, the realism of Kamakura, the genre art of Edo—all are as much alive today and as much a part of Japan's art in this generation as in any past generation. I believe that we should now look back into our art, and that Japan should undertake a cultural mission and introduce her art to the world. In that connection I can assure the reader that every picture in this book is a part of our cultural inheritance. It is my sincere belief that people all over the world will gain in understanding from this view of Japanese art over the centuries.

—NAGATAKE ASANO

ARCHAIC PERIOD
Before 552

Where did the Japanese people come from?...Facts and legends....The mysterious bronze bells of the Yayoi period. ...The giant tombs called *kofun*. The gay, energetic, varied world of the *haniwa* people and their horses, ducks and birds....The important role of the horse in a prehistoric age....The use of iron and the development of the sword which becomes both the instrument and symbol of power.

	HISTORICAL CHRONOLOGY		*ART CHRONOLOGY*
Before B.C. 4500	*Non-ceramic culture prevailed*	*Before B.C. 4500*	*Chipped stone implements (hand-axe, points, and blades)*
c. B.C. 4500 -250	*Jōmon culture emerged: primitive hunting and fishing communities, pit dwellings, shell mound burials*	*c. B.C. 4500*	*Jōmon (rope-marked) pottery, dogū (totemistic figurines), stone formations*
B.C. 660	*Legendary date for founding of Japan under Emperor Jimmu*	*c. B.C. 300*	*Yayoi wheel-made pottery, bronze implements, wood tools*
c. B.C. 300 -c. A.D. 300	*Yayoi culture emerged, due to continental stimulus: wet rice agriculture*	*c. B.C. 100*	*Ceremonial bronze swords and bells (dōtaku), dolmen burials*
c. B.C. 100	*Pre-Yamato tribal groups*	*c. A.D. 100*	*Han dynasty bronze mirrors*
A.D. 57	*Record of envoy from Japanese "kingdom" of Nu to Han court (first mention of Japan in a non-Japanese source)*	*c. 260*	*Possible date for founding of Ise shrine dedicated to the Sun Goddess, ancestral deity of the Emperor*
c. 150	*Small tribal groups developed into federation*	*c. 400*	*Large tombs, some with painted decorations, gold and stone ornaments; decorative horse trappings; armor; cylindrical clay images (haniwa); haji (domestic) and Sué (funerary) pottery*
c. 285	*Traditional date for the introduction of writing from Korea (Probable actual date c. A.D. 450)*		
c. 300	*Yamato government established; Kofun culture: clan (uji) organized society, Shintō religion, hereditary occupational guilds (be)*	*c. 438*	*Tomb of Emperor Nintoku*
		c. 500	*Haniwa became more elaborate*
478	*Emperor Yūraku's memorial to the Sung Court*		

Note: Because there is no clear evidence regarding exact dates in prehistoric Japan, there is some overlapping in the chronologies and texts of the Archaic and Asuka periods.

THE BEGINNING

The specific origins of the ancestors of the present Japanese people are lost in the mists of time. Yet there is evidence that some of the islands of the Japanese archipelago were inhabited by primitive man as early as the Pleistocene period a million years ago. Later, some five thousand years before Christ, a culture was created known as Jōmon. The Jōmon people left examples of a distinct type of pottery characterized by a coiled rope pattern and created many strange figurines called *dogū*. They were in the shape of people and animals, and are believed to be representations of their gods.

These early ancestors of the Japanese people lived in a beautiful world in miniature. Sharply-etched peaks rose from gentle wooded hills. Fertile valleys formed a green mat to the sea. All was crowned by the towering perfection of Mount Fuji. Deer, bear, and boar roamed the wooded slopes. The coastal waters sheltered shrimp, langouste, eel, octopus and an abundant variety of fish. From the high snows sparkling streams became swift rivers and blue lakes. Springs, hot and cold, flowed from the hills.

Nature left a permanent imprint on Japanese culture. Shintō, the first form of worship, is

18

based upon awe, respect and affection for the elements. Forces for good or evil were believed to live in the wind, the rain, the mountains and the sea. With the abundance of water, the Japanese came to revere cleanliness; the ritual cleansing, *misogi,* became a part of their worship.

The early legends of Japan telling of the birth of the islands were part of the Shintō form of worship, known as "the way of the gods." They tell of the miraculous creation of the islands by Izanagi and Izanami who were the parents of the Sun Goddess, Amaterasu, and of many gods and goddesses who controlled the moon, fire, wind and other elements of nature. As the early tribes slowly moved from nomadic hunting to agriculture, the legends of the origins of Japan were handed down from one generation to another by word of mouth.

◄ *Stylized doll-like figurine, dating from the neolithic period, has thick neck and curiously slanted eyes.*
► *Abstract scoring in clay distinguish this* dogū. *Decoration common to the period includes lines, dots and circles.*
▼ *Concave face with large nose and unique eye treatment becomes apparent in close-up detail of figure at right.*

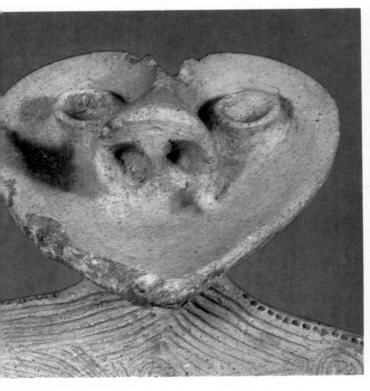

THE MYSTERIOUS BELLS

Bronze was the first metal to enter Japan. From it, in the first or second century before Christ, bell-shaped objects were created and on them were etched hunting and fishing scenes, outline pictures of tortoises, lizards, birds and other animals and insects indigenous to the islands. Some archeologists have conjectured that they were used in religious ceremonies, others that they were simply objects of beauty or wealth. The bell-shaped bronzes, each with a curved handle, range in size from less than a foot to four feet in height. Their shape may be of Chinese or Korean origin for similar objects have been found in northern Korea, but the illustrations showing vivid scenes of life in the Yayoi period are distinctly Japanese.

Bell-shaped bronze dōtaku stands 18 inches high. On it are primitive drawings depicting animals, hunters and (at bottom left) early agricultural workers. In detail, a prehistoric hunter aims an arrow from his short bow at a wild boar.

The most complete record of a distinctive early Japanese culture and the one that teaches most about life in the late Archaic period is the giant tomb called *kofun*. Built in the shape of a gigantic keyhole, these elaborate burial chambers were surrounded by hundreds of hand-fashioned clay-cylinders called *haniwa*. Of simple design in the earliest tombs, within a short time these cyl-

inders became more detailed and representational. The clay figures that decorated the tombs of rulers showed not only the various types of people then residing in the islands, noblemen, foot-soldiers, priestesses and peasants, but also their horses, chickens, deer, ducks and birds.

In character and design these figurines were wholly Japanese. Rich in humor and variety,

THE HANIWA PEOPLE

Family group includes head of woman with necklace and huge earring. Patriarch is resplendent in carefully trimmed beard. Young man wears highly-stylized hair cut. House below is from the late haniwa *period of sculpture which is characterized by the simplicity of its geometric form.*

they show people of varying stations and different professions. In addition to people, houses of the period can be reconstructed from the clay miniatures of them which were placed on top of each tomb. Many of the farmhouses in Japan today are constructed in the same fashion. As mirrored by the *haniwa* figurines, the people of Japan lived in an active and energetic society.

THE COMING OF THE SWORD

Iron replaced bronze in Japan during the second and third centuries A.D., and the sword evolved into the most important weapon of conquest. Throughout Japan hordes of aborigines were driven north by men with swords as the early clans began to form. Because of its great value, for there were few swords in these early days, the weapon became important not only for defense and conquest but also as a ceremonial object. It appeared as one of the earliest symbols of power in Japanese tradition. The son of the gods Izanami and Izanagi, Susa-no-o, used an inferior sabre to kill an eight-forked serpent and within the serpent found a great sharp sword. This sword, it is said, became part of the Imperial Family regalia and a symbol of power.

Warriors usually carried a short sword with a large, easy-to-grasp handle, but they also knew and used a longer blade. Fighting men of the period may at times have carried both.

By A.D. 300, most of the tribes had been joined in a confederation and, as the aborigines were conquered, many groups moved from the coastal settlements to the plains in the region of Yamato. As the welding of tribal groups continued and a military tradition developed, these early Japanese became well enough organized to extend their control to a part of southern Korea.

Prehistoric haniwa *building with large chimney may have been used as ancient forge for making warrior swords.* ▼ *Ceremonial sword is shown alongside figure of* haniwa *warrior. Size is approximately same as an actual sword.*

◄ *Warrior, wearing helmet, armor and long gauntlets, draws his sword. First swords arrived about first century A.D.*

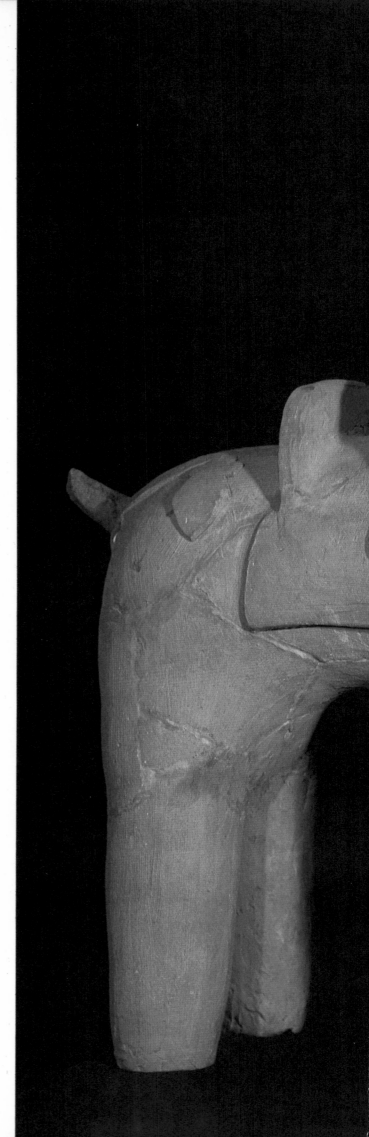

THE FIRST HORSEMEN

As important as the sword to the prehistoric Japanese was the horse. The small, sturdy Japanese steeds probably came from Mongolia via Korea. There is no record of just when horses first arrived in Japan, but there must have been great influx between the beginning of the bronze period and the early Asuka period. The indications of this are the drawings on the mysterious *dōtaku* bells, which show primitive hunters on foot, and reproductions of clay *haniwa* horses usually shown with saddle and bridle.

The beauty of the clay *haniwa* horses was celebrated in early legend. The *Nihon Shoki* (first chronicle of Japan) recounts the tale of a horseman called Hakuson who while riding by moonlight met a strange horseman mounted on a handsome red charger. Hakuson rode alongside and the rider of the strange horse, divining his wish for the red steed, stopped and exchanged horses. Happy at having such a wonderful horse, Hakuson rode home and placed him in the stable. The next morning his beautiful red horse had become a *haniwa* horse of clay. He went back along the trail which led him by the Honda Imperial tomb and found his own horse standing among the clay *haniwa* horses.

Reddish brown haniwa *horse stands ready for mounting. Figure leading him represents peasant of prehistoric Japan.*

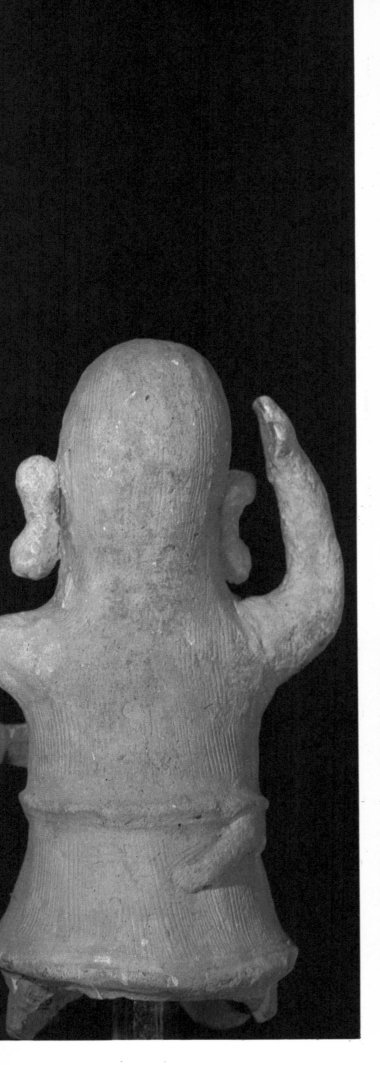

THE DANCING MEN

That dancing was an important part of the life of the early Japanese is vividly shown in the action and emotion of these highly distinctive, beautifully articulated dancing men. Earliest historical accounts indicate that dancing was an important part of the burial ceremonies. It was an important activity at early festivals celebrating the planting or reaping of crops and was probably an integral part of rituals relating to fertility and magic.

The *haniwa* figurines show important class distinctions. Some men represent nobles, others warriors and peasants. Clothing ranges from loose balloon-legged trousers (*hakama*) with tight-fitting jackets worn by men to woven skirts and narrow-sleeved blouses (completely unlike the loose kimonos worn later) for women.

There is nothing derivative from other cultures in the simple, gay figurines. They can be termed a natural expression of the Japanese.

◄ *Three dancing men show distinctly different* haniwa *types. Man on left may be noble, others peasants. They range from one to two feet in height. Haniwa sculpture often shows men in dance attitudes which may have religious meaning.*

Bird in flight makes decorative handle for jar (tsubo). Sculpture is Sué-type pottery of the late kofun period. ◄ Priestess or dancer has rouged lips and face paint. Body pattern scored in clay may indicate ceremonial robes.

PAINTED FACES
—FAMILIAR ANIMALS

The sculptors of this era favored simplicity of form yet achieved an emotional quality, often of awareness. This may be seen in the eyes of the figurines, though the eyes were simple holes cut directly into the clay. But their use of color was realistic. Pink and red designs were sometimes painted on faces and bodies just as later histories tell of people who painted themselves.

Domestic animals were an important part of life in this prehistoric period for, in addition to chickens and dogs, men are sometimes shown with a trained falcon on the arm. In reproducing familiar animals in clay, *haniwa* artists strove for the essential quality rather than the external detail. Birds, ducks, dogs, horses, monkeys, bears, deer and chickens—even though the representation is more abstract than realistic—are readily recognized.

Monkey looks at world through hollow eyes. Considered one of the most important examples of haniwa animals.

ASUKA PERIOD 552-710

 The nation begins to take shape among the clans in the Yamato valley.... Missions to Korea and T'ang China bring back Confucian ideas and Buddhist piety....The beginnings of a written language.... The devout and intellectual Prince Shōtoku emerges as the first great national leader. He inspires Japan's first Buddhist culture.

HISTORICAL CHRONOLOGY		ART CHRONOLOGY	
552	King of Paekche sends a Buddha image and sacred writings to Japanese emperor; traditional date for introduction of Buddhism into Japan	593	Shitennōji and Asukadera construction begun
562	Conquest of Japan's Korean holdings by Silla	603	Bodhisattva in meditation, wood sculpture, Kōryūji
587	Civil war, Prince Shōtoku and the Soga family are victors; Prince Shōtoku vows to build Shitennōji (first temple built by court)	607	Hōryūji built; bronze Yakushi Buddha is the main image
594	Proclamation of Buddhism as the state religion; rise of the Soga family in government	622	Chūgūji tapestry showing Prince Shōtoku in paradise
604	Seventeen-article constitution; official use of Chinese calendar	623	Sculptor Tori casts bronze Shaka trinity, Hōryūji
607	Dispatch of first mission to Sui China	c. 650	Four guardian kings, Hōryuji
645	Taika reform; overthrow of Soga family; Court adopts Chinese administrative institutions to insure its control of the country	666	Hōryūji sculpture of Miroku bodhisattva in meditation
663	Defeat of Japanese army in Korea	7th C.	Kudara Kannon statue, Hōryūji; Tamamushi shrine: scenes from the life and manifestations of Buddha
702	Promulgation of Taihō legal code	c. 710	Paradise mural Hōryūji
708	First coining of copper money	8th C.	Gigaku masks

ANCIENT JAPAN

Japan began to show evidence of becoming a political entity about the same time the Christian era started in the western world. The traditional date is A.D. 57, when, according to contemporary Chinese sources, an envoy from the King of Japan arrived in Loyang, the capital of China, and received, from Emperor Kuang-wu, a cordon and a seal—apparently a form of diplomatic recognition. These contacts with the mainland continued and became a major influence in the development of Japanese civilization.

The first outlines of what can be called a state began to emerge during the fourth century in the fertile central plains of Yamato. The dramatic and eternal evidence that there was some kind of primitive political organization comes from the huge tombs (*kofun*) found in and around the valley. In each tomb is the body of an emperor surrounded by the bodies of tributary chieftains—an arrangement that apparently reflected the growth of clans.

Life centered at a riverside spot in the valley called Asuka, where the Imperial palaces were built. The Yamato chieftains not only sent their envoys to China, but were able to establish suzerainty over part of southern Korea.

However, conflict rather than cooperation was the rule among the early clans, and out of these struggles one clan, the Soga, emerged as dominant during the sixth century. In 592 Umako, the head of the Soga clan, had the Emperor Sujun assassinated and raised his niece to the throne as Empress Suiko. He then maneuvered the appointment of the Empress' nephew, Prince Shōtoku, as regent. Shōtoku, a devout young Buddhist intellectual, became one of the great figures in Japanese history.

Umako was no intellectual, but he seems to have felt that the future of Japan—and of the Soga clan—lay with the spread of new knowledge, and he recognized that Shōtoku could be agent of this transformation. Umako remained in the background and apparently allowed Prince Shōtoku a free hand in spreading Chinese learning and Buddhist piety.

Perhaps the most important political achievement attributed to this learned and intelligent ruler was the promulgation of an early constitution. It was essentially a list of maxims which should not be considered laws in the western sense, except perhaps for Article 12, which refers to the power of this early government to collect taxes. It read:

"Let not the provincial authorities or the old local nobles levy taxes on the people. In a country there are not two lords; the people have not two masters. The Sovereign is the master of the people of the entire country. The officials to whom he gives power are all his vassals. How can they, as well as the government, presume to levy taxes on the people?"

◄ *Golden seal in shape of curly-haired animal is believed to be one given by Chinese Emperor Kuang-wu to the Japanese envoy to China in A.D. 57. Above is impression of seal.*

Men with swords and shields decorate bronze mirror. Such mirrors, kept in the Shintō temples, have religious origins.

This provision indicated the beginning of the influence of the great empire of Han China, in which the power of local lords or governors was taken over by a strong central government.

Article 16 of Prince Shōtoku's constitution reflected the already great importance of rice cultivation and of the silkworm. It also contained the primitive elements of a planned economy. It read:

"Let the people be employed (to pay government taxes) at seasonable times. This is an ancient and excellent rule. Let them be employed therefore in the winter months when they are at leisure. But from spring to autumn, when they are engaged in agriculture or with the mulberry trees, the people should not be so employed. For if they do not attend to agriculture, what will they have to eat? If they do not attend to the mulberry trees, what will they do for clothing?"

Most of Prince Shōtoku's maxims were far

more general. They bespoke harmonious relationships between lords and peasants. He equated lords and fathers as leaders of their people. The three treasures to be most prized by the people were Buddha, his "law" and the monastic orders. And these were to be taken as the supreme objects of faith in all countries.

He enjoined superiors to behave with decorum lest their inferiors become disorderly. He urged ministers and functionaries to attend the Court early in the morning and retire late, since the whole day was hardly enough for the accomplishment of the business of the state. In general, the constitution asked that the people lay aside local differences and accept Imperial rule in order to achieve social and economic harmony for the common good.

Yet all did not go smoothly during the Asuka period. China destroyed the Korean kingdom of Paekche which was allied to Japan, and wiped out Japan's foothold on the peninsula. A civil war involving the Imperial succession erupted and ended with the victory of the Emperor Temmu. He placed his Court in Fujiwara, near Asuka, and here a second Buddhist culture emerged around the Imperial Palace.

Evidence of Japanese writing is shown along edge of mirror dated A.D. 503. It includes forty-eight Chinese characters.

PRINCE SHŌTOKU

So many virtues and achievements are attributed to Prince Shōtoku that he has almost become a legend. But he was without question a historical man. He was born in 572 and he died in 622. He became regent of Japan in 593 at the age of twenty-two during a time when the teachings of Buddhism were beginning to spread in Japan. The formal introduction of Buddhism is put at 538 or 552 when the Korean kingdom of Paekche sent the Japanese Emperor some Buddhist images and sacred writings. Under Prince Shōtoku's benevolent guidance Buddhist culture flourished in Japan for the first time. He ruled by example as well as precept. He was a devout and learned Buddhist, and wrote commentaries on the sacred scriptures of Buddhism,

the sutras. He promoted the construction of monasteries, seminaries, shrines and chapels. Among these were the monasteries of Hōryūji near Nara and Shitennōji in Osaka. Painting, sculpture and architecture were also encouraged.

In political matters Prince Shōtoku patterned his rule after the illustrious Han dynasty in China. He sought to bring the quarreling clans under a central administration. He set up hierarchic ranks in the Imperial Court in an attempt to substitute merit and experience for heredity. A so-called constitution of seventeen articles setting forth appropriate rules of public conduct is attributed to him. Prince Shōtoku was in effect a sage-ruler whose influence was seminal in the development of his country.

▶ *Revered Prince Shōtoku stands with his two sons, Prince Yamashiro Ōe and Prince Ekuri, in posthumous portrait.*

Manifestation of Buddha dives from cliff to offer his body to starving tigress and her cubs.

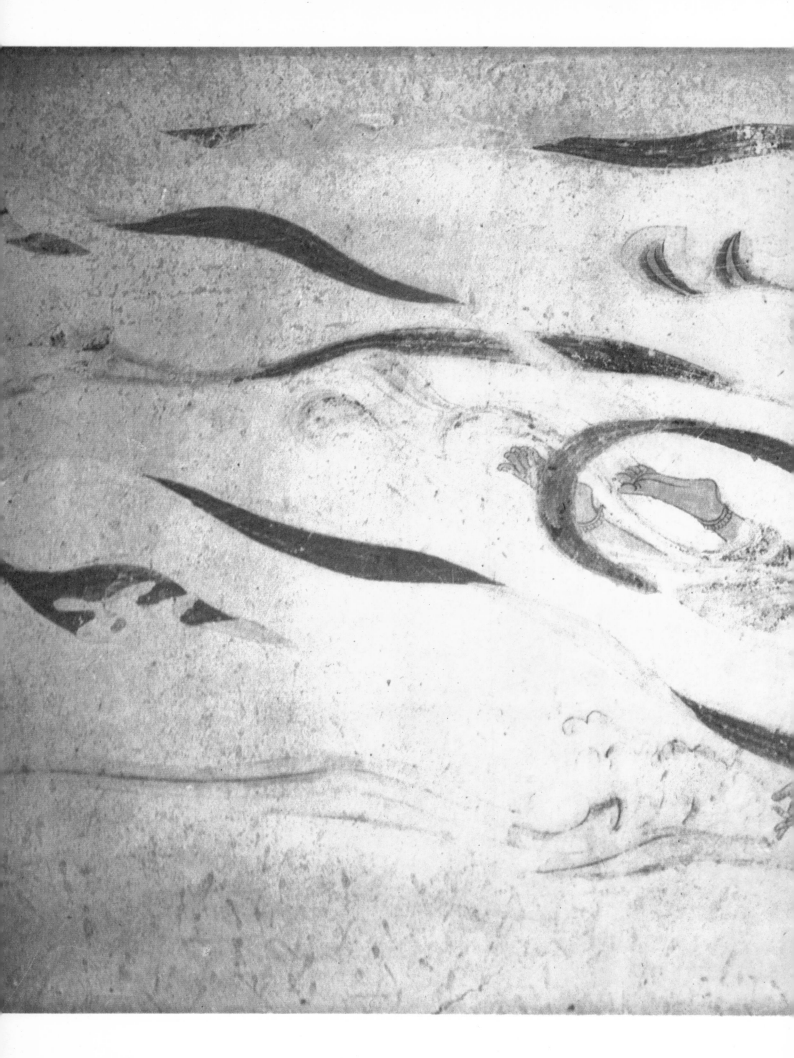

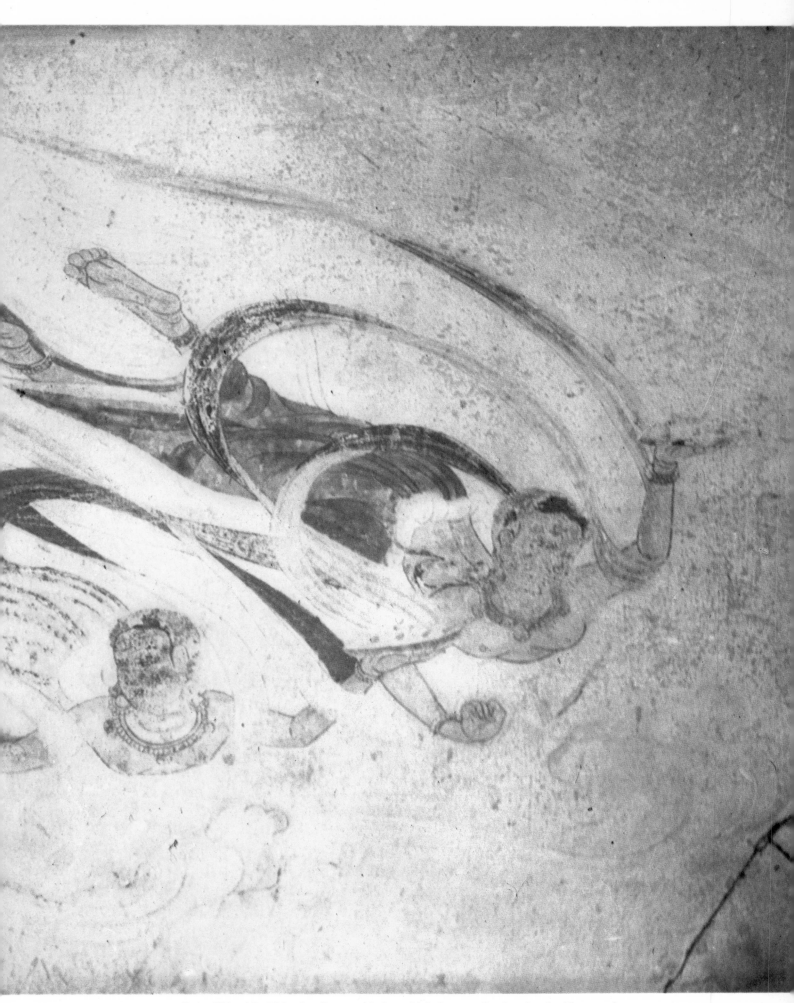

Flying angels decorate wall in Hōryūji. This detail escaped fire which destroyed other invaluable murals.

Priceless silk embroidery illustrates paradise where Prince Shōtoku is believed to have been reborn after his death.
▶ *Flying without wings, airborne Apsarases are shown on streamer of gold-plated copper used for tonsure ceremony.*

◄ *Spiritual contemplation is suggested by hand touching chin in this exquisite Buddha of the Future called Miroku. Statue dated in the 14th year of Empress Suiko's reign.*
► *Eyes almost shut, mouth gently smiling, the face expresses ideal of inner harmony.*

Smiling mask for dramatic pantomime called Gagaku. Presentations were accompanied by music and performed in temples.

GAGAKU

Gagaku, a distinctive type of Japanese music and dance based upon Chinese music, developed between the seventh and ninth centuries. Performance consisted of masked dancers representing different characters and formally accompanied by a small orchestra consisting of five to eight instruments. They included drums, flutes and a string instrument similar to a mandolin called a *biwa*. The music was slow, high-pitched and graceful. Dances included military routines in which swords and spears were often used. Performances were limited to the Court and the nobility. The word Gagaku can be freely translated as "elegant music."

NARA PERIOD 710-794

A new capital is constructed in a fertile and beautiful valley and a whole culture is devoted to the veneration of the life of Gautama Buddha.... Monasteries, nunneries and temples flourish.... The first stirrings of a literature produce histories and a poetry anthology.... Buddhism and the rigid Chinese pattern of centralized rule dominate the government.

HISTORICAL CHRONOLOGY		ART CHRONOLOGY	
710	First permanent capital established by Empress Gemmyō in Nara	c. 710	Fujiwara supported Kōfukuji established at Nara (Hossō sect); Tachibana shrine Hōryūji
712	Official chronicle Kojiki (Records of Ancient Matters)		Construction of Kasuga shrine
713	Fudoki (Survey of the Provinces)	718	Yakushiji (est. 680) moved to Nara, with bronze Yakushi trinity as main image
720	Official chronicle Nihon Shoki (Chronicles of Japan)	729-49	Kako Genzai Inga kyō scrolls (illustrates sutra of the past and present incarnation of Shaka)
728	Sutra of Golden Light (Konkō myō saishō ō kyō) sent to all provinces		
729-49	Tempyō period	734	Kōfukuji statues of eight guardian devas
741	Official provincial monasteries and nunneries (kokubunji) established	739	Yumedono (hall of dreams) erected at Hōryūji
754	Ganjin, Chinese Buddhist priest, arrives in Japan	742-52	Construction of Tōdaiji, Nara (Kegon sect); possibly founded in 733
c. 759	Compilation of Manyōshu, poetry anthology	747	Statue of Fukūkenjaku kannon, Tōdaiji
764	Defeat and death of prime minister, Fujiwara Nakamaro; Buddhist priest Dōkyō becomes prime minister	752	Great Buddha (Roshana butsu) dedicated at Tōdaiji
770	Empress Shōtoku dies; Dōkyo is exiled	756	Emperor Shōmu's belongings dedicated to Tōdaiji, preserved in the Shōsōin (built 760)
781-806	Kammu is Emperor; prestige of the throne high	759	Tōshōdaiji founded by Ganjin (Ritsu sect)
794	Capital is moved from Nara	c. 763	Sculpture of Ganjin

THE GOLDEN AGE OF BUDDHISM

Prince Gautama Siddhartha, the historic Buddha, was born in India. His teachings spread over China and reached Japan where they found highly receptive soil.

Buddha taught four truths that lead to perfect knowledge and enlightenment or the state of Nirvana. 1) In all life there is suffering. 2) Suffering is caused by desire. 3) Suffering can be ended because the cause is known. 4) The way to end suffering is to follow the eight-step path: right conduct, right intent, right speech, right knowledge, right means of livelihood, right effort, right mindfulness and right meditation.

These principles evoked a sympathetic response in the Japanese temperament; nor was there any real conflict with Shintōism. Both the Court and the peasant found comfort in a belief in non-violence, in the sacred nature of all living things and in an overall plan for each life.

Buddhism became the symbol of the age. A new capital had been erected in a fertile valley of the Yamato basin. It was called Heijō, or Nara, and was modeled after the capital of T'ang China. Nara soon became the center of advanced Buddhist doctrines. Learned monks taught the words and deeds of Gautama. Two famous temples, the Hōryūji and Yakushiji, had been standing in the peaceful valley. Now monasteries and nunneries sprang up in the wooded hills. In the Court, learning and the arts blossomed. They bore fruit in the form of the first two historical chronicles of Japan, the *Kojiki* and the *Nihon Shoki*, and in the *Manyōshū,* the first great collection of poetry, which included early works of a distinctive Japanese flavor.

Colorful, delicately-wrought statues were created for the temples and the Court. Chinese scrolls depicting the details of his life were adopted by Japanese artists to show Gautama from a Japanese point of view. The Emperor Shōmu built a fifty-three foot statue of Buddha, the Vairocana image. The capital was ablaze

The Buddha, it is written, was born from the side of the Queen Maya as she reached up to a branch in her garden.

Seated with his father and mother, the young Prince Gautama is entertained by dancers. Below he sees a dying man.

After the Buddha was born, it is told, he took eight steps and said: "In all the world, I am the only honored one."

with color in brilliant painted roofs, decorated columns and painted temple doorways. Sculpture, painting, handicrafts, music and literature all flourished in the Buddhist climate.

But it was also a period of unrest. Crop failures and heavy taxes plagued the peasantry. The promotion of Buddhism might have been in some degree a conscious attempt to pacify the discontent. If so, it did not succeed significantly. The old Japanese land tenure system was based on extensive private holdings of semi-autonomous clans. Influenced by the Chinese pattern of small holdings owned by individual farmers paying taxes to a central government, the Nara nobles embarked on a program of dividing the land into small family farms.

The plan faltered because there was not enough desirable land for all who wanted it. But a greater barrier to success was the tax burden. Three types of taxes were levied: a land tax payable in rice; a produce tax on products other than rice, such as fish or silk, and payable in the product itself; and a labor tax which the farmer or his sons paid by serving in the military or on civil works projects. To evade these onerous taxes and to keep from starvation, many small farmers abandoned their holdings and became serfs on large estates. As more land was repossessed by the aristocracy and the church, the tax burden became increasingly heavy on the small landholders. They had no choice but to sell, mortgage or abandon their lands.

The favored Buddhist monasteries became large landholders and an increasingly important part of the central government. During the latter part of the Nara period, the monk Dōkyō became chancellor and Buddhism spread from the capital throughout the provinces. But Dōkyō failed in his attempt to assume control over the throne, and the Buddhist influence in the Imperial Court gave way to the influential nobles of the rising Fujiwara family.

Stories of Buddha tell how, as a youth, he saw his young cousin push down an elephant. Gautama said he had done evil.

Strong and active as a youth, Gautama practiced traditional Eastern wrestling, closely related to sumō wrestling today.

To show his natural strength, Gautama lifted the elephant, saying it is more important to lift up than to push down.

An expert at archery, Gautama successfully wills his arrow to pierce the targets, using a great bow only he could draw.

Sitting with his wife, Gautama is unhappy, for he feels the need to go out into the world to find himself.
▶ *At baptism of Gautama, gong is struck to erase evil desires. Vessels on heads contain water for tonsure.*
▼ *Gautama leaves home, wife and wealth to go out into the forest. Attendants go to inform his family.*

THE BURNING BUDDHA

Fire was often the theme of the Buddha's sermons. In one sermon he spoke of the world aflame; of all men on fire with passion. hatred, infatuation, birth, old age, sorrow, grief and despair. He explained that all are blinded by these flames and that when men understand the holy way the fire will be extinguished within them; that they will no longer be blinded by the attractions of the flames and will be free of the fires of passion and desire.

In a parable the Buddha told a story of the affection between an old man and a hare. When the old man was starving, the hare threw himself into the flames that his body might supply food for his friend. Transformed, he became a vision of the Buddha; the old man then realized that within the small body of the hare lived the unselfish spirit of the Buddha.

Out riding one day, Gautama sees a sick man. Shocked by man's suffering, he dedicates his life to serving humanity.

Coming upon remains of a dead man, Gautama realizes the same end awaits all; nothing on earth is permanent.
▶ Amidst flames an incarnation of spiritual Buddha shows that the physical body can be sacrificed for common good.

58

THE DEATH OF BUDDHA

As he approached eighty years, the Buddha became ill and his disciples felt that death was near. But he explained that he had much to accomplish and his entrance into Nirvana must be postponed. He therefore arose from his sickbed.

Three months later, he lay down to die with his faithful disciples around him. Even though it was winter, it is said the trees burst into bloom. The Buddha told Ananda, his cousin and favorite disciple, that, although he was departing this life, the truth which he taught was the real master and would be with the world always.

As his soul entered Nirvana, it is said the earth shook and thunder rolled across the sky.

▲ *Death of Gautama shows him giant size, mourners small. Under Sala trees, near River Vati, he entered Nirvana.*
◄ *A royal minister weeps while court lady mourns the death of the great spiritual leader of India, China and Japan.*
► *Complete calm is expressed on Buddha's face as he lies amidst grieving bodhisattvas, archats and his disciples.*
▼ *A demon and a lion grieve at the death of the Buddha. All life, human, animal, and supernatural is represented.*

THE WORLD OF BUDDHA

Japanese painters and sculptors, deeply influenced by Buddhist art from China and India, peopled an entire paradise with guardians, generals, bodhisattvas, Apsarases (musical angels), priests, goddesses, demons, disciples and images of the Buddha.

When the Emperor Shōmu decreed that each province should build both a pagoda and a temple, these images appeared throughout Japan. Inside the temples great figures of the Buddhist faith were installed. The Emperor himself built a figure of Vairocana called Daibutsu that towered over all others in the nation. It rose fifty-three feet from the ground. Casting it took decades, and all the Buddhist world knew of its preparation. A huge building was constructed to house the monument, and it is recorded that ten thousand Japanese, Chinese, Korean and Indian monks attended the dedication ceremony.

In fashioning the sensitive and colorful figures that peopled the Buddhist world, the artists of the Nara period added a new dimension to the figures made of bronze or of wood by previous generations. They created statues of clay heavily painted with lacquer. By removing the core of the clay and replacing it with a lightweight wooden frame, these dramatic sculptured figures could easily be carried in religious processions.

Within the Buddhist temples many arts were blended. Music and the dance were practiced and taught as part of the religious ritual.

▶ *Protruding fangs, curly hair, necklaces and loincloths indicate the non-Japanese character of these unique goblins on pedestal which holds god of medicine in Yakushiji.*
◀ *Divine wrath is portrayed in face of this warrior demigod, one of the deva kings who guard temple and Buddhism from evil influences. Statue is of clay painted with lacquer.*

Symbolic snake is held by this almost life-size figure of a Sakara. Certain characteristics, such as his dark face, indicate an Indian influence which entered the country before and during the Nara period.

HEIAN PERIOD 794-1185

An era of elegance, sensitivity and good taste....Buddhist and Chinese influences continue, but indigenous Japanese tendencies emerge....The aristocracy with Fujiwaras as Regents become spokesmen for Emperors....The Cloistered Emperors....The Emperor who was abducted....A lady writes the first novel....The warrior class shows its strength.

HISTORICAL CHRONOLOGY		ART CHRONOLOGY	
794	Permanent capital Heian-kyō (Kyoto)	816	Kongōbuji built at Koyasan (Shingon sect)
801	Defeat of Ainu in northern Honshū	851	Enrakuji built on Hieizan (Tendai sect)
805	Dengyō Daishi introduces Tendai sect of Buddhism	860	Iwashimizu Hachiman shrine built
806	Introduction of Shingon sect of Buddhism by Kōbō Daishi	890	Statues of Shintō goddess, Nakatsu-hime, and of Hachiman as a Buddhist priest placed in Yakushiji, a Buddhist temple
858	Beginning of Fujiwara family rule through the emperor	9th C.	Red Fudō, attributed to Kōbo Daishi, Kōyasan; statue of Rōben Sōjō, founder of Tōdaiji
901	Sugawara Michizane exiled to Kyūshū		
972	Kūya, a proponent of Amida Buddhism, dies	10th C.	Painting of Amida and the twenty-five bodhisattva, attributed to the priest Genshin
c. 1002	Lady Sei Shōnagon writes Makura no Sō-shi (Pillow Book)	1053	Construction of Hōōdō (Phoenix Hall) of the Byōdōin; the temple had been convert-ed from use as a residence in 1052; statue of Amida by Jōchō
c. 1008-20	Lady Murasaki Shikibu writes Genji Monogatari (The Tale of Genji)		
1051-62	Nine Years' War in northern Honshū	1064	Figures of twelve generals carved by Chō-sei and placed in Kōryuji
1083-7	Three Years' War in northern Honshū	1069	Munezane's pictorial biography of Prince Shōtoku
1086	Emperor Shirakawa abdicates and es-tablishes "cloister" government (rule by a retired emperor)	1086	Painting of the death of Buddha
		c. 1100	Animal caricature scroll by priest Toba Sōjō
1095	Soldier monks from Enryakuji march through Kyoto	1140	Shigisan Engi Emaki (Legends of Mt. Shigi), attributed to Toba Sōjō
1159	Heiji War: the Minamoto are defeated	12th C.	Painting of Fugen bodhisattva; Genji monogatari scroll by Fujiwara Takayoshi; picture scroll, Ban Dainagon, by Tokiwa Mitsunaga
1167	Taira Kiyomori appointed prime minister		
1175	Hōnen Shōnin establishes Jōdo (Pure Land) sect of Buddhism		
1180-5	Gempei War: Taira defeated by the Minamoto clan led by Minamoto Yoritomo		

◀ *Komoku-Ten, one of four guardians of the Buddhist world. This powerful statue is an early work from northeast area.*
▼ *Banished unjustly, Sugawara Michizane holds bamboo stick bearing his version of false charges on Mt. Tempai-san.*

EMERGING ARISTOCRACY

With the transfer of the Court from Nara to Heian-kyō, now the city of Kyoto, the rigid Chinese pattern of government shifted slowly to a system more suitable to the Japanese temperament. The Emperor Kammu had two good reasons for ordering the move from Nara: Buddhism had so penetrated the old capital that it threatened to absorb the government; the new regime needed a new locale to make a fresh start toward solving the burgeoning problems of the fast-growing country.

In the new capital the Chinese influence lingered, but attitudes changed about the court language and the failing tax system. A syllabary based upon the use of simplified Chinese characters to represent Japanese sounds developed into a native writing system. A widespread breakdown in Chinese governing and taxgathering techniques became apparent.

It was a period of growth in every direction,

Jealous of Michizane's influence, the Fujiwara family succeeds in having him exiled to the island of Kyūshū. Armed police (upper right) stand on shore as his colorful houseboat is rowed away. Sea monster looks from water at lower left. ▼ Happy childhood of Sugawara Michizane shown as he participates in archery contest with other members of nobility.

but the most distinctive quality of this growth involved two factors seldom mentioned in a nation's history: good taste and sensitivity. These qualities ran through law, literature, painting, speech, poetry and diplomacy. They were even part of the governing process.

The country was avid for learning. Two new Buddhist sects were brought from China by Japanese priests. The first was the Tendai sect introduced by Saichō. He built his temple on Mount Hiei and supplied leaders and teachers to the new nation.

The priest Kūkai founded the Shingon sect and built a monastery atop Mount Kōya. He was a remarkable man: aristocrat, scholar, calligrapher and painter. Through control of body, speech and mind, he thought, came Buddhahood. There were only two directions in which mankind could go, he taught—up toward Buddha or down toward hell.

The austerity of the monasteries was protected by lay attendants who guarded inmates against intrusion of liquor, women and robbers.

The Emperor Kammu, although encouraging both of these men, did not allow religion to dominate his government as the Buddhists had dominated earlier periods. But dominance was to come soon from another direction—from the very aristocracy that surrounded the Court.

A powerful family, the Fujiwara, was rising. Their power derived from vast landholdings and they exercised it as regents to the emperors. To insure their influence, they supplied their daughters as concubines and consorts to the Emperor and to the other nobles. This practice resulted in the flooding of the Imperial Court with Fujiwara progeny. Among them were crown princes who soon became emperors. The grandfather, uncle or father-in-law often became the power behind and the spokesman for the titular Sovereign.

Fujiwara control was weak in the periphery of the Empire, particularly in the north where Japanese warriors were pushing back the aborigines and carving out estates from the wilderness. Inevitably, a conflict developed between the pioneers, who built private armies to extend and defend their lands, and the noble absentee landlords, who remained in the capital. The Fujiwara were also weakened by monks who controlled great estates and the military men who lived on and protected them.

Saddened by exile, Michizane reminisces of happier days
while viewing court costumes sent to him by the Emperor.
▼ In a flashback to his youth, Michizane is seen studying
with his father in the family's formal Japanese garden.

Dying in exile, Michizane was buried where oxen stopped with his remains. Sorrowful villagers prepare his grave.

Shintō goddess Nakatsu Hime Zō, wearing elaborate robes of court lady, was worshipped at Hachiman-gu shrine in Nara.
▶ *Expressing his anger at evil, one of the Twelve Heavenly Generals of Buddhist world stands guard at Kōryūji in Kyoto.*

SHINTŌ GODDESSES AND BUDDHIST GENERALS

The fusion of Shintō with Buddhism which started in the Nara period developed fully in the Heian. Many Buddhist temples adapted Shintō gods as local manifestations of the everlasting Buddha. Shintō shrines erected Buddhist temples within their walls. Cooperation between Buddhist and Shintō leaders was popular.

The close relationship between the two cults is apparent in the prayers of the retired Emperor Shirakawa to the Shintō god of war, Hachiman, and his making an offering of copies of the Buddhist scriptures.

THE FIRST NOVEL

The first novel in any language and one of the greatest was written by Lady Murasaki Shikibu about the year 1000 and was called *The Tale of Genji*. The book recounted the young manhood of Prince Genji, handsome, generous and amorous. It followed his adventures in Court with a series of ladies. He becomes wiser as he grows older, and the novel ends when Genji is thirty and is considering the priesthood.

But *The Tale of Genji* was more than a romantic love story. It was full of insights into the character of the principals. It re-created the sights, sounds, manners and morals of Heian court life. Lady Murasaki had a unique ability to project a feeling of awareness and of beauty, to isolate the moment of pathos, to find oblique ways of illuminating the complex life of her characters.

When Lady Murasaki created her novel, the Japanese written language had been developing for more than two hundred years. It was now possible to write in rich and subtle images and she made the most of it.

A few years earlier *The Pillow Book* had been written by Sei Shōnagon, another court lady of intelligence and wit. It was a series of impressions of the small pleasures enjoyed by people of educated tastes—the feel of heavy silk cloth, a rustle of autumn leaves, the color of dying flowers. Her book was gay, filled with what the Japanese call *okashi*, a smile suddenly expressed and quickly gone.

Both books tended to show how deeply refinement and awareness of beauty had entered Japanese life. These qualities spread from the aristocracy to the warrior class—many soldiers were known for the excellence of their poetry—and eventually became the heritage of the nation.

Warrior hero, Minamoto Yoshiiye, determined the position of his enemy by observing direction of flying wild geese. ◄ Encamped near battlefield, Yoshiiye hears reports from aides. He was called Hachiman Taro, son of the God of War. ► Warrior during Three-Years War in full battle regalia. Visor of helmet could be moved down to protect face.

THE WARRIORS

The medieval warrior was well equipped and highly trained for warfare. One of his two most important weapons was the bow. Made of bamboo, it was reinforced with rattan binding and varied in length from six to seven and a half feet, taller than the warrior himself. Arrows about three feet long carried hawk feathers and were held in a quiver across the back.

His battle sword was of tempered steel with a slightly curved and convex blade. The right to wear a sword was a great honor, for with it came certain privileges and responsibilities. To the early warriors of Japan, it was a way of life and a way of death.

THE CLOISTERED EMPERORS

The end of domination by Fujiwara regents and their women was hastened by a unique interlude known as government by cloistered emperors. This was a practice under which, typically, an emperor would abdicate in favor of a fully controllable puppet, such as his young son, and become a priest. Then, free of excessive ceremonial burdens and protected from palace conspiracies, he could rule more effectively from his ecclesiastic cloister. As time went on, matters became quite complicated; behind the titular Emperor there was not only the cloistered Emperor but also several additional retired emperors, plus regents, warriors and priests. After nearly one hundred years the system strangled itself.

Its end came with a struggle over succession to the throne in 1156. One claimant for the throne was backed by the Fujiwara and the Minamoto. The other, who had the larger following, was supported by the cloistered Emperor and the rising Taira clan.

The cloistered Emperor and his Taira supporters won and dealt harshly with the Minamoto opposition. The (*Continued on page 90*)

Foot soldier leads general on charger at end of scroll showing abduction of ex-Emperor Go-Shirakawa; Emperor Nijō.
► *Inside Sanjō Palace in Kyoto, the rebel general, Minamoto Yoshitomo orders ex-Emperor into waiting carriage.*

Forcing the Emperor and Empress into a carriage, abductors escape from the palace, fighting loyal guards to the death.

A grim escort surrounds the royal coach. Curtains on the carriage are drawn to hide ex-Emperor Go-Shirakawa and Princess.

Flames roar through the palace as the insurgent forces plunder the buildings and massacre Go-Shirakawa's loyal supporters.

In center of picture, soldiers of the rebel forces cut off head of loyal defender, while others search for more victims.

Confused nobles reach the palace to find that the gate has been locked. Unable to enter, they mill around helplessly.

While the rescuers attempt to force their way into the palace court, the conspirators escape with their captives.

(*Continued from page 78*)   leader of the Minamoto clan, Tameyoshi, and his son, Yoshitomo, were both captured. The ex-Emperor, Go-Shirakawa ordered the son to decapitate his father. He refused. But a Minamoto retainer, declaring that it would be an insult for a Minamoto to be executed by a Taira, beheaded Tameyoshi and killed himself.

Yoshitomo was able later to avenge his father's death when he assisted a young Fujiwara nobleman in one of the most dramatic exploits of Japanese history—the forcible abduction of ex-Emperor Go-Shirakawa from his palace.

The plot was simple and direct. As general of the left gate and chief of the palace police, Fujiwara Nobuyori allowed Minamoto Yoshitomo to bring his own army into the palace grounds without causing alarm. The Emperor, along with Princess Jōsei Monin, was lured into a closed carriage and driven out of the left gate of the Palace while at the right gate the Emperor's supporters clamored for entrance. Minamoto Yoshitomo then had the Palace fired. But the Emperor soon escaped in disguise. Nobuyori and Minamoto Yoshitomo were tracked down by the Taira clan and killed.

Rebellious troops of Nobuyori and Yoshitomo are pictured preventing court officials from rescuing royal treasure.

Later, the young Emperor Nijō, abducted with ex-Emperor Go-Shirakawa, escapes, disguised as a lady in waiting.

Armed monks, protectors of the Buddhist monasteries, descend from their hilltop retreat to observe a ritual dance drama.

Noted for his ethical conduct, Taira Shigemori was Kiyomori's eldest son. His early death hastened fall of Taira power.

FALL OF THE TAIRAS

In an age of continuous intrigue, Taira Shigemori was considered to be a man of high ethical principles. He was a resourceful warrior as well and became commander-in-chief of the army, responsible only to the Emperor and to his father, Taira Kiyomori. He often acted to modify the unjust measures of the tyrannical Kiyomori.

Shigemori did not live to see the final downfall of the Tairas whose prestige and power he had helped to create. Tired of the spying, treason and immorality of the Court, it is said that he prayed for death. He was only 42 years old when he contracted a fever and died. With all temperate control gone, his impetuous father took the Taira clan down the path of destruction. The instruments of that destruction were to be the Minamoto, the rivals he had tried to annihilate.

KAMAKURA PERIOD 1185-1333

The redoubtable Minamoto Yoritomo makes himself the Shōgun—or generalissimo—of Japan, establishes the first Shōgunate....The valor of the samurai, plus a timely hurricane, thwart two massive attempts by the Mongol, Kublai Khan, to invade Japan....The priest Eisai introduces Zen Buddhism....Poetry is rarefied and painting is realistic.

HISTORICAL CHRONOLOGY		ART CHRONOLOGY	
1185	Provincial constables (shugo) and stewards (jitō) appointed by Minamoto Yoritomo's military headquarters in Kamakura	c. 1200	Minamoto Yoritomo portrait by Fujiwara Takanobu
1191	Introduction of Zen Buddhism (Rinzai sect) from China by Eisai	c. 1200	Jigoku zōshi scrolls (hell scrolls)
1192	Yoritomo given title of Shōgun, location of Shōgunate (bakufu) in Kamakura	1203	Niō (guardian figure) statues by Unkei
1199	Death of Yoritomo, power of Shōgunate assumed by Hōjō family	1219	Kitano Tenjin scrolls (biography of Sugawara Michizane)
1205	Hōjō shōgunal regency begins	1233	Portraits of thirty-six poets by Fujiwara Nobuzane
1221	Jōkyū disturbance; Kyoto initiated anti-Shōgunate movement fails	1247	Zuishinteiki scroll (portraits of nine imperial guards)
1226	Court noble, Fujiwara Yoritsune, is selected Shōgun	c. 1250	Heijimonogatari scroll
1232	Law code Jōei shikimoku issued (Kamakura law code)	1252	Bronze Amida image erected at Kamakura
c. 1250	Heike Monogatari (Tale of the Heike) written	After 1281	Nachi waterfall painting
1253	Nichiren sect of Buddhism established	1282	Engakuji established (Zen sect)
1262	Shinran, founder of Pure Land (Amida) sect, dies	1293	Mongol Invasion scroll by Tosa Nagataka
1274 and 81	Mongol invasions	c. 1296	Tengu Sōshi scrolls (goblin scrolls)
1289	Death of the traveling priest, Ippen	1299	Life of Ippen Shōnin scroll by Eni
1325	First official embassy to China since T'ang dynasty	13th C.	Statue of Jizō by Unkei and Kaikei, Tōdaiji; statue of Kūya chanting prayers, Rokuharamitsuji
1333	Hōjō regency ends; imperial rule under Emperor Go-Daigo	c. 1300	Hōnen Shōnin scroll by Tosa
		1309	Takashina Takakane's scroll of miracles which occurred at Kasuga shrine

Minamoto Yoritomo was the first permanent Shōgun. He wears ceremonial sokutai robe rather than general's uniform.

THE SEEDS OF FEUDALISM

Out of the bitter struggle for supremacy between the Taira and the Minamoto, the two military giants of the twelfth century, came a new kind of government based on the rule of military men headed by a military dictator—the Shōgun. The man responsible for this development was Minamoto Yoritomo who became Generalissimo, or Shōgun, of the first Shōgunate, or *bakufu,* in Japan.

In theory the Shōgunate operated as the military arm of the Emperor's government. Actually, its control included the Emperor and the Imperial Court. Yoritomo's power spread to the appointment of land stewards and constables throughout the nation, and through them the Shōgunate enjoyed tax collection privileges.

So began, in Kamakura, the era of medieval Japan. Until then, the development of the country had been relatively peaceful. But the Kamakura Shōgunate planted the seeds of feudal government, and for the next five hundred years there would be a series of changing rulers, rebellions, revolts, and civil wars. The greatest hero and builder of the feudal system was the vigorous, clever, power-hungry warrior, Minamoto

Yoritomo, who experienced his first battle at the age of thirteen and rose to rule Japan when, in 1185, he inflicted a crushing defeat on the powerful Taira family.

Yoritomo was a product of an age that bred frontier warriors, knights on horseback dependent upon themselves and family alliances, to beat back the aborigines who threatened from the north. He was bred in an age in which hand-to-hand combat among warriors of equal rank was traditional. He could, and did, proudly announce the exploits of his ancestors as he accepted a challenge to do battle. Many of the dramatic episodes in later Japanese plays were based on the sometimes heroic, sometimes treacherous actions of this intrepid leader. Many of his battles were fought by his brother Yoshitsune, whom he betrayed and forced into committing suicide.

One early story tells how Yoritomo's life was saved in battle by the Zen nun Ike and how he was later able to return her kindness by sparing the life of her son. This incident may have influenced his later protection of Zen Buddhism. When the Zen priest Eisai returned from China a full-fledged Zen master, he moved from Kyoto

to Yoritomo's capital in Kamakura, where he became a great favorite among the rugged, hard-living warriors of the Shōgunate. Much of the influence Zen was later to have throughout Japan began at this time. When Yorimoto died, the Hōjō regents who followed him extended their favor to Eisai and continued to promote the study of Zen in both Kamakura and Kyoto.

This Zen priest who brought a philosophy to the warriors also brought one of the great cornerstones of Japanese culture. From China he carried seeds for the planting of tea, and he preached that this nonintoxicating beverage was a health-giving elixir that would bring long life to those who imbibed it.

Though many good things had come to the Japanese from China, their contact with the mainland was soon to be most unpleasant. The Great Khan, Kublai, sent envoys to Japan demanding capitulation and threatening invasion should the rulers refuse. The Shōgunate did refuse, and the result was two invasions. The Mongols were repulsed, but at such a cost to the Kamakura treasury that it never recovered.

Weakened financially, the Shōgunate fell to a clique led by the Emperor Go-Daigo, who at the close of the Kamakura period attempted to restore the power of the Imperial household.

◀ *Equestrian sketch portrays one of cloistered emperor's royal mounted guards as he sits astride a spirited horse.*
▼ *Names of these ex-emperor's bodyguards are inscribed above each portrait. Bows and arrows were the guards' only arms.*

VISIONS OF HELL

Ideas of heaven and hell were written down with great imagination and vividly painted beginning in the Heian and extending into the Kamakura period. The Buddhist priest Genshin was the first to preach and write of the many horrors of hell. His book describing the tortures of hell and the rewards of paradise became the most important religious work of its time.

He told of hells where sinners were forced to attack one another, cutting each other's bodies until only bones remained, or where the flesh was slowly sliced off the victim by demons. This was a hell of repeated torture. Sinners, after being cut up, were quickly revived only to have the painful process begin again. Into this hell murderers were cast. In other hells people were slowly devoured by loathsome insects, boiled alive, ground between stones, or endured a rain of sharp, flaming swords.

The joys of paradise were as countless as the horrors of hell. They included the joy of being born again, of being welcomed into the company of saints, of becoming a supernatural being, of beholding the Buddha, of wearing rich garments, and of living a life of everlasting pleasure.

▲ *Sinners, who have descended into hell, burn in river of fire representing one of the many horrors they must face. Buddhism offers many hells for evil doers. Punishment for murder, stealing, adultery was vividly portrayed in scroll.*

POETRY AND PAINTING

► *Poets were revered in the Kamakura period. Kodai-no-ki-mi wrote excellent verse. She was a member of the nobility.*
▼ *Winner of a national poetry contest, Taira Kanemori is immortalized on the famous Scroll of Thirty-six Poets.*

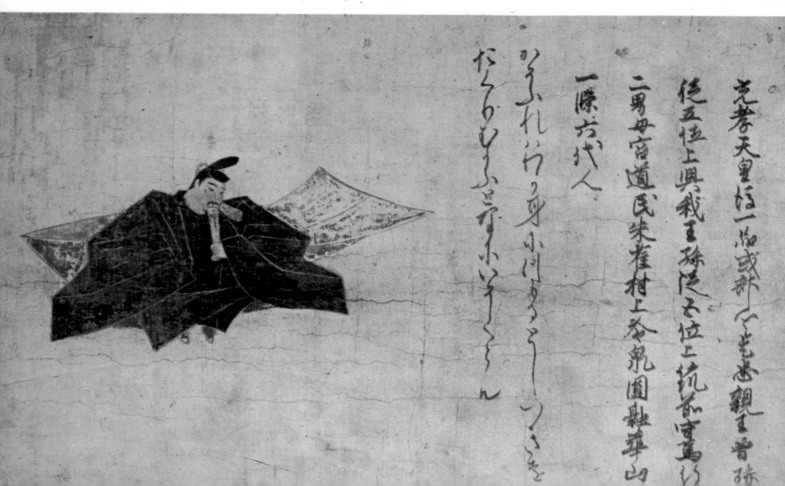

光孝天皇恒一品式部卿之忠惠親王曾孫

従五位上興我王孫陸奥位上筑前守篤行

二男母宮道民朱雀村上於泉圓融華山

一際六代人

つれつくの身の小川ありつゝみ

たくむらふうよろい

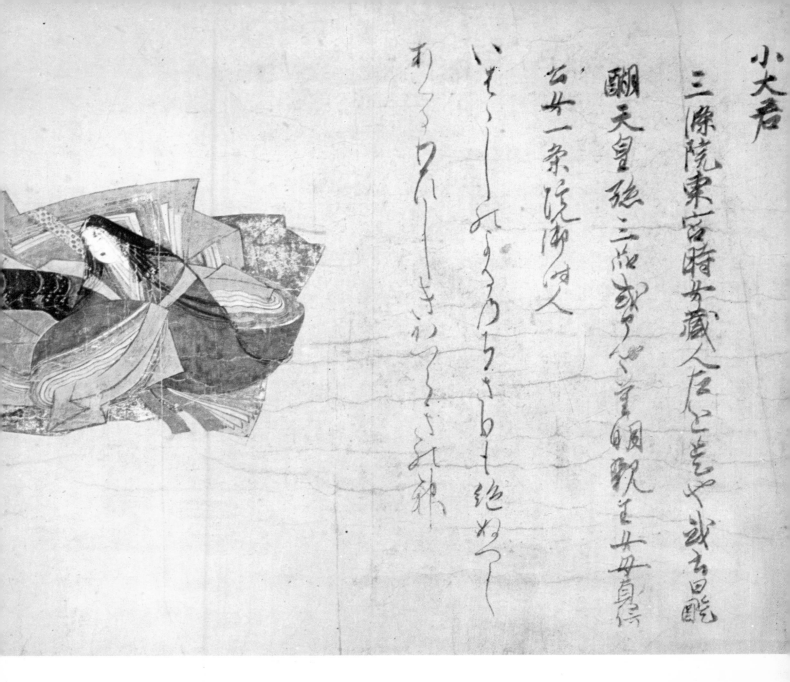

Highly rarefied poetic thought and highly realistic historical painting were the artistic hallmarks of the early Kamakura period.

The key to Japanese poetic expression is called *yūgen*. The nearest translation of this is thoughts that are remote, deep and mysterious; concepts never simple or easily understood. The early poets strove for an impression of an emotion. They expected the reader to feel the sentiment engendered by the poem and even to understand a meaning although the meaning was not expressed in words. *Yūgen* is something like the effect of looking through a mist, or finding many meanings in the sound of a single flute playing in the night.

If poetry in early Kamakura was remote and mysterious, painting was not. Great historical events were realistically recreated in lengthy hand scrolls which unrolled from right to left. These storytelling picture scrolls became the foundation for the *yamato-e* (true Japanese) style of painting. Subject matter included narratives of recent wars, the rise and fall of noble families and the dramatic exploits of warriors.

Inventive artistic techniques showed the blur of rolling carriage wheels, and flames were said to be painted so realistically that one could feel the heat. The passage of time was often indicated by a mist or cloud formation above or below the action shown in the scrolls. Called *kasumi*, the cloud pattern often consisted of semicircular clouds joining or separating two scenes.

Poetry and painting were the special concern of the Court or the aristocracy but were not confined to them. They were taken up by the new warrior class and spread throughout Japan.

The early styles in poetry and painting begun in Heian came to full fruition in Kamakura.

105

Attacking Mongols, troops of the Emperor of China, first captured the islands of Tsushima and Iki then landed on Kyūshū.

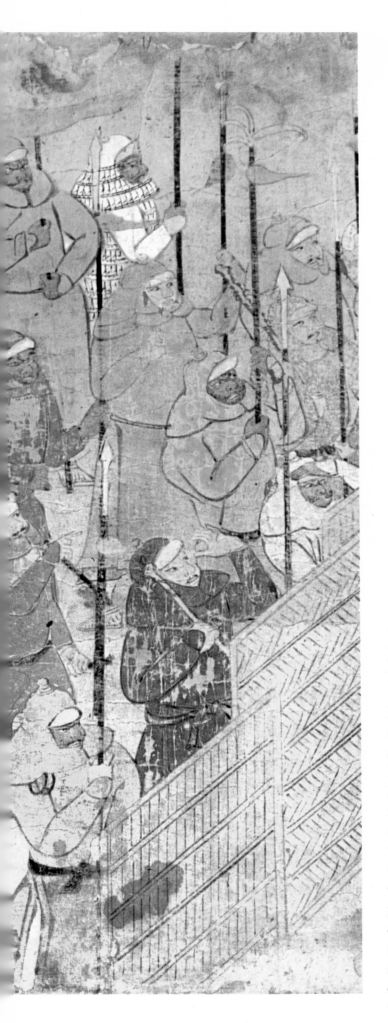

THE MONGOL INVASION

While the Japanese warrior class, through the Kamakura Shōgunate, was establishing a comparatively stable state with strong and orderly government, the Mongol warriors of Genghis Khan were overrunning Asia and spreading chaos. In 1259, Kublai Khan, grandson of Genghis, became Emperor of China and five years later established his capital in Peking. He lost little time in making it clear that Japan was the next object of Mongol ambitions. He started by sending envoys to Japan demanding surrender under pain of invasion. At first the Imperial Court in Kyoto was inclined to compromise. But when the ultimata were presented to the Shōgunate, these proud warriors rejected the Mongol challenge with contempt. The envoys of the Great Khan were insulted and expelled; one mission was even executed. The demand for unconditional surrender was to be met with unconditional resistance. (*Continued on page 111*)

肥後國竹崎五郎兵衛季長
生年二十九

Famous warrior Takezaki Suenaga attacks Mongol bowman, though his horse is wounded. Fireball explodes in air at center.

Behind thick bamboo screens used as mobile shields, Mongol warriors retreat as the Japanese press their counterattack.

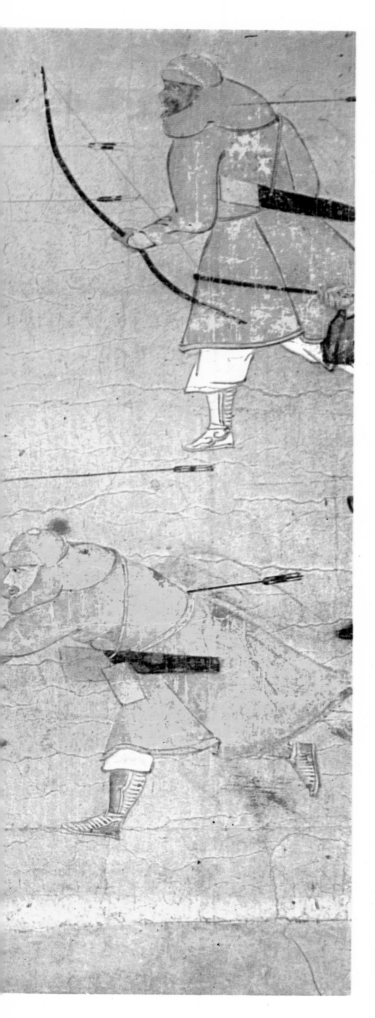

(*Continued from page 107*) Kublai's plans included heavy dependence on the kingdom of Korea which, after a long struggle, had submitted to Mongol suzerainty. The southern tip of Korea was only one hundred miles from the main Japanese islands. Seafaring was unknown to the Mongols, and an invasion of Japan was possible only by using Korean ships and sailors. The Koreans became collaborators of the Mongols, though unwillingly.

The first Mongol invasion got under way in November 1274. It consisted of an armada of about 300 large and 450 small vessels carrying 15,000 Mongol and Chinese soldiers, 8,000 Korean troops, and 7,000 Korean and Chinese sailors to man the boats.

The invaders sailed for Hakata Bay, which was deep and well sheltered, on the northern coast of Kyūshū. They captured the islands of Tsushima and Iki after wiping out the small Japanese garrisons, which resisted to the death. They then headed for the mainland and made landings at Hakata, at Hakozaki and Imazu.

The Japanese resisted fiercely. But their

great skill was in single, hand-to-hand combat; they were no match for a massed army, trained in close-formation maneuvering and armed with powerful crossbows, moving shields, and cata- pults which could throw heavy missiles and fire balls. If the Kyūshū defenders could have held out until the arrival of reinforcements, the Japanese might have won by sheer force of num-

bers. But the situation was saved from another source. A severe storm arose and the Korean ship captains persuaded the Mongol generals to re-embark their troops to avoid the risk of be-coming isolated on shore. The fleet straggled back to Korea after heavy losses by drowning.

Kublai, without delay, sent another mission demanding Japan's submission, and the Shōgun-

Riding through heavily forested woodland, warrior Suenaga leads the hastily organized Japanese cavalry to the battleground.

ate again rejected the insult with speed and decisiveness. This time the military planning of both sides was on a grander scale. The Mongols were determined not to be repulsed twice, and they took their time with their new preparations. The Japanese made full use of this respite.

The Shōgunate set about mobilizing the nation's manpower and wealth for defense. At one point serious consideration was given to taking the offensive by building a fleet capable of attacking the enemy's bases. This was finally rejected as beyond the Shōgunate's resources, but a fleet of small and maneuverable warships was constructed to act as a coastal guard.

It was decided that the focal point of Japanese defense efforts was to be the construction of a stone wall ten feet high along the shore of Hakata Bay in northern Kyūshū, where the invaders were again expected to strike. The purpose of the wall was to prevent or hinder a landing, and to make it impossible for troops that got ashore to move in massed formation. It took five years of work by impressed labor to complete the wall. The garrisoning of this defensive barrier was also a tremendous enterprise. Soldiers had to be trained, not only to defend the wall, but also to man both ends of it, where the enemy might be tempted to concentrate his assaults.

Charging into battle, vanguard of one hundred warriors is led by Shiraishi Rokurō. Streamer carries regimental crest.

Meantime the Great Khan proceeded relentlessly to put together what turned out to be the greatest overseas expeditionary force the world had yet seen. He set up a special high command, the "Office for the Chastisement of Japan," to coordinate what was becoming a much more complicated operation than the first invasion.

Kublai had subjugated the Sung rulers of southern China, and he promptly commandeered their fleet. It was assigned the task of transporting and provisioning an army of 100,000 men, most of them Chinese from the defeated Sung forces. The hapless Koreans, still suffering from the aftereffects of the first invasion, were or-

dered to double their previous effort. At first the King of Korea pleaded uselessly with Kublai to abandon a second attempt. Then, in the hope of receiving favored treatment, he reversed himself and proposed that Korea take a leading role. In the end, Korea became responsible for ships carrying 40,000 Mongol, Korean and North China troops.

The Great Khan ordered the attack to begin on January 4, 1281, but it was not until June that both fleets were able to move in coordinated fashion. The objective was again Hakata Bay and the first attacks were again made on the islands of Tsushima and Iki. *(Continued on page 118)*

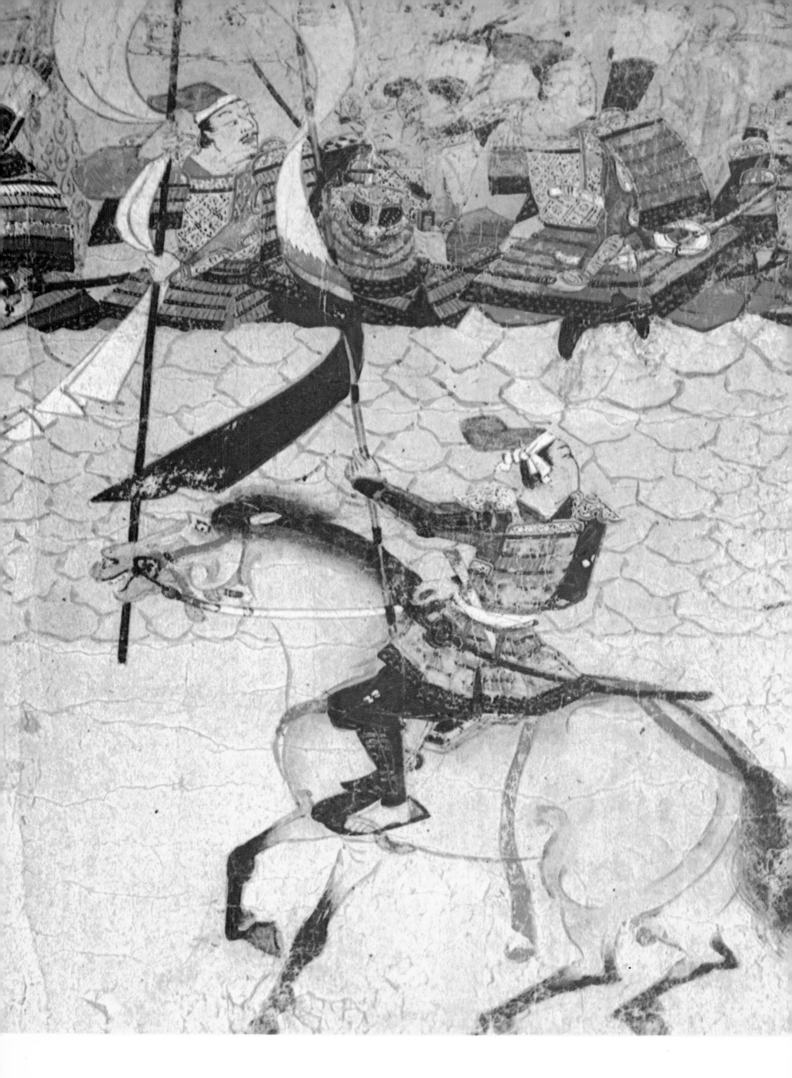

菊池次郎長

As bulwark against second invasion, Japanese built high stone wall shown here. When Mongols landed, Japanese were ready.

(*Continued from page 115*) This time the force on Tsushima was well prepared and it repelled the attack; Iki, however, was taken.

On the mainland the invaders landed in great numbers. But for the defenders matters went more or less according to plan. The stone wall was not successfully breached. Whenever the enemy forced an opening, the Japanese were able to plug it up. The pressure at both ends of the wall was heavy, but the defenders not only held firm but were able occasionally to press the attack. The Japanese fleet of small, fast and easily maneuvered coastal vessels inflicted significant damage on the lumbering enemy transports.

For seven weeks the line held. Then the weather intervened again. A violent hurricane blew up over the shores of Kyūshū and raged for two days. When it subsided, the Great Khan's armada had been battered into uselessness. At least half the Chinese force of 100,000 were drowned

Climax of fighting in second Mongol invasion comes when Japanese hero Suenaga boards ship to kill Mongolian leader.

or cut down as they tried to re-embark. The mixed force from Korea lost about one-third of its men. Japanese victory was decisive. The hurricane became known as *kamikaze,* or divine wind. The episode became a great patriotic epic in which the national deities, through the divine wind, saved the sacred soil of Japan from pollution. Shintōism, especially its worship of the Sun Goddess and Hachiman, enjoyed a revival.

Whether or not the Japanese could have continued their resistance during the second invasion and won without the help of the weather must remain a matter of speculation. Fighting morale could not have been high in the Korean staging areas or among the Khan's Chinese troops, themselves only recent victims of Mongol conquest. This must undoubtedly have been in sharp contrast with the spirit and valor of the Japanese fighting men, to whom defense of their country was practically a religion.

But the martial glory of the Shōgunate and its warrior vassals was short-lived. Now the economic strains began to show. Not until Kublai Khan died, in 1294, did Kamakura become convinced that another Mongol invasion would not be attempted and that the nation could safely begin demobilization. Japan had maintained a state of war or readiness for war over a period of twenty years. The warriors who had faithfully served the national cause demanded compensation and reward. (The warrior Takezaki Suenaga supported his claim with these picture scrolls which he had painted in color commemorating not only his own valor but also the exploits of other heroes. The scrolls depicted scenes on both land and sea in great detail.) Many of the warriors were deeply in debt to merchants and money lenders. Some had sold off their fiefs to classes that operated outside the relationship between the feudal overlord and the warriors and thus threatened the stability of this relationship.

The Shōgunate was virtually helpless in the face of these pressures. Its own resources had been seriously depleted. The war had been victorious, but it had been a victory of defense, and there was no booty to be distributed.

The Shōgunate resorted to desperate measures. It prohibited the foreclosure of mortgages on warriors' estates and the collection of debts by merchants. Such devices, however, created bitterness and confusion without solving the problem. It was the beginning of the end of the Kamakura Shōgunate.

◄ *In first invasion, Japanese were aided by fortunate typhoon (kamikaze) which sank most of Mongol fleet.*

▼ *Grisly aftermath of war is shown when Suenaga brings heads of Mongol generals to Japanese headquarters.*

RELIGION SPREADS

The people of Japan were weary of fighting. As the Shōgunate consolidated its power, they welcomed the precarious peace that settled over the country. Roads were opened and men and women traveled by horseback and palanquin, with their armed retainers preceding on foot, to the towns to shop for pottery, lacquerware and metalwork. The towns grew rapidly, most of them around the large monasteries and shrines, or alongside fine harbors.

Out of this direct contact between priests and the people came a mass religious movement. No longer was Buddhism to be confined primarily to the nobles of the Court in Kyoto and the leaders of the Shōgunate in Kamakura.

A religious fervor based upon a single precept swept the country: that escape from the terrors of hell and assurance of salvation could come

To ease his wife's birth pains, a husband asks village priest to pray. Prayers were answered, according to scroll.

from faith in the compassionate manifestation of the Buddha called Amida; that those who called upon his name and believed could enter the paradise of the Pure Land. This simple path to salvation was followed by another concept, which also made thousands of converts. It was led by an intelligent, stubborn priest named Nichiren. Instead of one Buddha concept, he taught the trinity of Buddha: the historical Bud-

dha whose body was transformed, the universal Buddha which is the "law", and the Eternal Buddha of compassion and bliss. By acceptance of the trinity and by calling upon them, enlightenment and salvation could be attained.

These two religious forms were easily understood by peasants, artisans, scholars, artists and samurai; throughout the provinces men and women joyfully accepted them.

空也上人遺跡
号市屋に云
一遍聖道場也

Scroll of priest Ippen Shōnin shows his travels through the countryside. He popularized dancing-praying ceremony.

THE TRAVELING PRIESTS

In Medieval Japan monks and priests traveled throughout the country carrying with them ideas of a better way of life. Some brought not only religious instruction, but also education and entertainment. The first of the great traveling priests, Kūya, lived between the years 903 and 972 in the mid-Heian period. He led the people in dance to the tune of a small bell which hung around his neck. Kūya attained great popularity and wrote many short poems which he taught the people to chant while dancing. His influence was especially wide in peasant villages, for his was a practical approach to the problems of daily existence. Although he led his followers in the dance in the evenings, he taught them to build roads, bridges and to dig wells, in the daytime.

Another early priest, Ryōnin, brought his message of hope through song instead of dance. His fine voice and great knowledge of traditional Buddhist music made him a popular figure.

Best known of all of the traveling missionaries was the devout but unconventional priest, Ippen. He combined the ideas of his predecessors by teaching that singing and dancing—as a way of worship—could bring enlightenment. Ippen believed that the Buddha was everywhere, and so he traveled up the mountains, over dusty roadways, waded through streams, slept in the open, finding manifestations of his master.

Traveling priest, Ippen, shown at top left, was a hero to the common people and saw many sights as he roamed the country-

side. Above, men and women swim in a river near Kyoto. This may be the earliest record of a Japanese woman swimming.

Ippen, carrying all his worldly possessions, takes his message of piety, love and honor to a village in Ōmi province.

PRECEPTS OF IPPEN

Ippen's simplicity, his energy and good humor made him almost a legendary figure throughout Japan. He taught simple, easy-to-follow rules for good conduct. Among his precepts were respect for the beliefs of others; reverence for the Buddha, his "law" and the priests; compassion; self criticism, but not criticism of others; avoidance of lust, greed and anger; trust in the law of love; and the repetition of devout prayers to evoke the grace of Amida.

MUROMACHI PERIOD 1333-1568

A period of restlessness and uncertainty.... The dual Emperors.... Portuguese are the first Europeans to arrive, bringing missionaries and guns....Saint Francis Xavier, the Jesuit, follows....The authority of the Shōgunate is weakened....Military leaders struggle for supremacy....Oda Nobunaga almost succeeds in bringing the country under one sword....The Nō drama appears.

HISTORICAL CHRONOLOGY		ART CHRONOLOGY	
1334	Emperor Go-Daigo resumed Imperial rule	1338	Ashikaga Takauji and Tadayoshi established ankokuji (temples of "a country at peace") in each province
1335	Ashikaga Takauji revolted against Go-Daigo		
1336	Rival emperor enthroned by Takauji	c. 1345	Painting of Zen priest Kanzan by Kaō Ninga
1336-92	Period of northern and southern Imperial courts	1347	Scroll of The Story of the Latter Three Years' War by the governor of Hida
1338	Takauji assumed title of Shōgun and established the Muromachi Shōgunate	1397	Kinkakuji (temple of the golden pavilion) erected as a villa at Kitayama by Ashikaga Yoshimitsu
1401	Diplomatic relations and trade opened with Ming China		
1443	Death of Seami, developer of Nō drama	c. 1400	Nō masks
1467-77	Ōnin Wars	1418	Studio of the Three Worthies, painted by Zen priest artist, Shūbun
1481	Buddhist priest Ikkyū died	c. 1460	Portrait of Zen priest Ikkyū
1543	Three Portuguese arrive at Tanegashima; introduction of firearms	1486	Sesshū's "longer" landscape scroll
1549	Arrival of Saint Francis Xavier in Kyūshū	1489	Ginkakuji (temple of the silver pavilion) erected as a villa at Higashiyama by Ashikaga Yoshimasa
1568	Oda Nobunga seized Kyoto		
1569	Christian missionaries granted permission by Nobunaga to carry on work	c. 1500	Zen rock garden made at Ryōanji
		1506	Death of painter monk, Sesshū
1570	Nagasaki port opened to foreign trade	c. 1550	Shuban-ron piece; portrait of Saint Francis Xavier
1573	End of Ashikaga Shōgunate		

THE DUAL DYNASTIES

Rule by the Shōgunate was not always smooth in medieval Japan. Court nobility was usually ready to rally around a strong emperor willing to contest its power. Such an emperor was Go-Daigo who, with a group of royalists, overthrew

Three samurai in elegant kimono eat rice from lacquer bowls while woman serves sake *from* hishaku, *a wooden container.*

the warrior Kamakura government in 1333. Though the powers of government were restored to the Court, the warrior chiefs continued to rule their own domains and to sit side by side in counsel with the nobility and the Emperor. The result was corruption and confusion.

Taking advantage of this situation, one of the Imperial generals who had aided the Emperor in gaining control of the government, Ashikaga Takauji, grew dissatisfied and, breaking away

from the Court, set up a rival Emperor from another line of Imperial descent and had himself appointed Shōgun. The conflict between the two Emperors of Japan and their courts, and the disputes over succession threw the country into civil war for more than fifty years.

Each man became his own defender. The high constables, who had been in charge of keeping the peace under the Shōgun, and the land stewards, who collected taxes, took matters into their

In kitchen scene, cooks prepare cormorant and carp. In foreground, vegetables are being prepared over charcoal stoves.

own hands and became true feudal lords with their own serfs, private armies and tax collectors. These lords, called *daimyo,* became virtual rulers of their own independent states.

The period was called *sengoku,* "country at war." But inside the autonomous domains established by the *daimyo* there was comparative tranquility and prosperity. The artisan and merchant classes developed under *daimyo* protection. Feudalism had arrived in Japan.

133

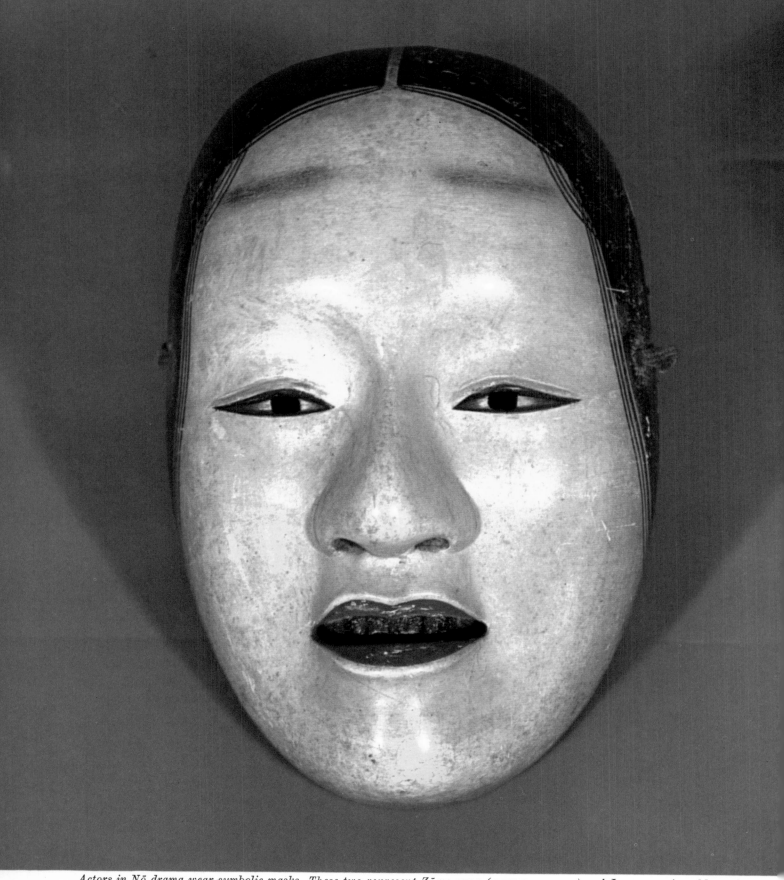

Actors in Nō drama wear symbolic masks. These two represent Zō-no-onna (a young woman) and Jo-no-men (an old man).

THE THEATRE OF NŌ

Greatest of the medieval arts to develop in the Muromachi period was the symbolic theater of Nō evolved by Seami, an actor, playwright, composer and critic. He created a theater of suggestion in which meaning was implied rather than stated. Masks were used to represent various types of people, and the drama behind the mask was projected by sophisticated and disciplined speech, gesture, dance, body movement and by the sheer intelligence of the actor.

▶ *Oda Nobunaga brought most of Japan under his control. When opposed by armed Buddhist sects he destroyed their political influence and their greatest monastery, Mount Hiei.*
▼ *Natural son of an Emperor, Ikkyū Sōjun became Zen priest. Many tales are told of his disregard for conventions.*

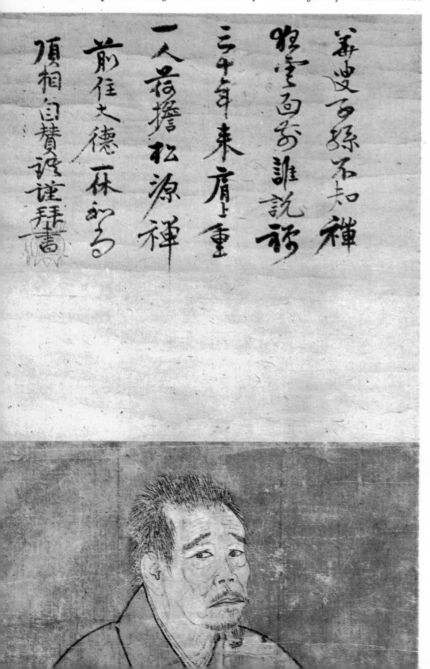

THE STORY OF RICE

The history of Japan is inextricably interwoven with the cultivation of rice. From the earliest beginnings of agriculture, when the prehistoric ancestors of the Japanese turned from fishing and hunting to land cultivation, rice has been the staff of life for the Japanese people.

The country is ideally suited for successful rice growing. The valleys of Japan are broad, flat and fertile, and of equal importance, are well watered by heavy spring and summer rains. And from the earliest times the resourceful Japanese successfully irrigated their fields in order to supplement the natural distribution of rainfall. Terracing, complete with retaining walls and facilities for drainage, reaches far back into Japanese history.

The earliest legends concerning the origins of the Japanese relate to the all important rice

Peasants engage in gay summer festival in front of rural Shintō shrine. Along with dancing, they pray for a good crop.
▼ In ancient ceremony, farmers ask the aid and blessing of the gods of nature before planting their rice crop.

crop. When the Sun Goddess, Amaterasu Ōmi-kami, was attacked by her brother Susa-no-o, god of the wind and sea, he, legend has it, wrecked her rice fields, ruthlessly tearing down the dams and ruining the crops. Further on, the tale tells dramatically how the frightened Sun Goddess sought refuge in a dark cave. With her departure, the light of the sun vanished from the world. Deeply concerned, other gods of heaven

In spring, fertility offerings of boiled rice are made to Shintō gods. Priest and assistants kneel before altar. ▶ Ground is worked by farmers until ready to receive the rice seed. Paddies are then flooded from storage dams.

and earth met before the entrance of the cave, hoping to lure the frightened Sun Goddess back into the world. Resorting to guile, they created a sacred tree and upon it hung a mirror and a jewel. Then one of the goddesses performed a vulgar but amusing dance. Hearing the mirth outside the cave, the Sun Goddess was naturally curious, ventured to the entrance and was struck by the beauty of the jewel and intrigued by her brilliant reflection in the mirror. Thus light was returned to the world.

Within this ancient legend lie all the elements of primitive beliefs based upon the realities of everyday life. The wind and the rain can destroy the rice crop; the sun in typhoon weather can be obliterated. And it is reasonable to assume that to bring back the sun, heartfelt ritual dances were held. The jewel and the mirror described in this tale became, with the sword, the three symbols of the Imperial Family.

For generations their ceremonies, prayers for sunny weather and for a good harvest, continued. Festivals of dancing and reverent meetings of the elders were held by the farmers of Japan to insure their food supply. But there was never enough rice for the (Continued on page 145)

Working in mud and water, women transplant the tender seedlings. In the background young musicians keep workers happy.

Using this ancient but ingenious foot-operated machine, farmers raise the water level to irrigate their rice paddies.

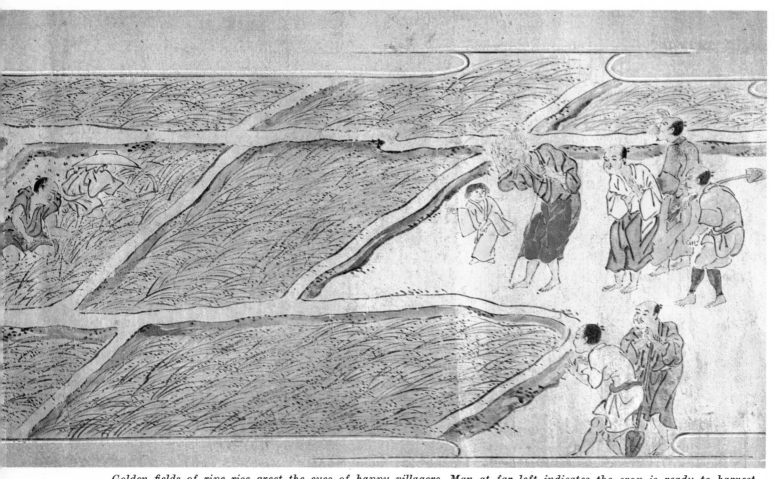

Golden fields of ripe rice greet the eyes of happy villagers. Man at far left indicates the crop is ready to harvest.
▼ *After harvesting, women husk rice, separate grains from the chaff, clean and pack it into bales made of rice stalks.*

Upper left is noble, next is samurai, below peasants, and at right is monk, merchant and artisan—all eating rice.

(*Continued from page 140*) fast-growing country. Men and women worked long hours planting the seedlings, then more hours, wading in mud up to their thighs, transplanting the shoots.

As the rice ripens, the patterns and colors of the countryside change. From chartreuse the fields become deep green and, as the rice becomes ripe, it changes to a warm, yellow brown.

Throughout its early history, Japan depended upon the rice crop for its wealth. The taxes of the country were largely paid in rice. The salaries for the samurai, who defended the lords and their domains, were traditionally paid in rice. Feudal lords and the clan leaders who preceded them, recognizing the importance of the farmers, made every effort to keep them from changing status.

▼ *Taxes were paid in rice. Farmers paid their taxes to the representatives of the* daimyo, *feudal lord of the province.*

145

THE SAMURAI SWORD

The creation of swords for warriors became much more than a craft by the fifteenth century. It was an art, perhaps even more respected than the art of painting. For the sword was not simply a weapon of offense and defense but was considered, quite literally, the soul of the samurai. To give up his sword was to give up his life.

The samurai carried not one but two swords.

146

His long sword was up to five feet in length and he carried a short sword to cut off the heads of his enemies or to commit *seppuku,* The samurai considered his sword to be of such great value, both for its spiritual and magical qualities and its actual economic value, that upon retirement to a monastery or in penance for some unfor- givable offense, he presented the weapon to be enshrined with other sacred relics in a temple or shrine.

The samurai dedicated himself to death in defense of his master and his honor. He lived a life of frugality and discipline. Rarely did he have any important material wealth except his sword.

◄ *Swordsmiths were the most honored artisans of their time. Final polishing shown here required great technical skill.*
▼ *Early stage of sword making shows primitive forge. Iron is being heated and shaped. The box is a primitive bellows.*

148

FIREARMS
AND CHRISTIANITY

A strange ship, larger than any ever seen in Japan, appeared in 1543 off the shore of Tanegashima in Ōsumi province at the southern end of the island of Kyūshū. It was large enough to carry a hundred men, who wore balloonlike trousers and short jackets. They spoke an odd-sounding and unintelligible tongue. The villagers were suspicious and resentful.

Accompanying the strange men when they came ashore was a Chinese, who could communicate with the chieftain of the village. He explained that they came from a distant land called Portugal. He warned that although they were wise in many ways they knew little of politeness or of etiquette as practiced by the Chinese and the Japanese. He assured the village spokesman that they were there only for the purpose of trade and would not harm the people.

The Japanese called them *namban*, meaning southern barbarians, just as the Chinese had called the Japanese barbarians at an earlier date and as the Portuguese themselves referred to non-Christians.

What brought the Portuguese was undoubtedly the already famous travel book written by Marco Polo, thirteenth century explorer, in which he told of the riches to be found in the islands called Zipangu, off the coast of China. In this fabled land, he wrote, gold was to be found in abundance—in fact, columns of gold could be seen in the palace, and windows were decorated with golden ornaments. The Venetian explorer had also written that valuable pearls were to be

Portuguese landed in Japan in 1543. Sea-going Japanese were intensely interested in Portuguese ships and navigation.

found in great quantities; they were so numerous that a pearl could be put into the mouth of each person when he was buried. Furthermore, the islands of Zipangu were independent of foreign powers, governed entirely by their own kings. Their religion was the worship of idols.

It was therefore understandable that Zipangu, or Japan, was the goal of many European expeditions, beginning with the first voyage of Columbus. The admiral from Genoa believed for many years that he had reached the rich and fabled islands of the East, unaware they were the poor, sparcely inhabited islands of the Caribbean Sea.

But the Portuguese, excellent sailors, had the fastest and best-equipped ships in the world.

They had learned from the voyages of Columbus and of their own Vasco da Gama. Their charts were the most reliable. They had already settled a colony at Goa and were trading along the China coast. So it was they who reached Japan first.

Their purpose was trade and the spread of Christianity throughout the world. They traveled under the authority of the King of Portugal and the Pope of Rome. Their critics in Europe and Asia felt that their trade policy consisted of exchanging the Christian faith for the wealth of the heathen countries. The criticism was not without validity. Some Portuguese traders were little more than pirates who committed many acts of violence, including the kidnapping of Chinese youths to sell as slaves.

▲ *Merchant at center has servants carry goods. Artist represented Japanese as being half the size of Europeans.*
◄ *Portuguese landing in Japan exchange trade goods at seaside village. Goods are placed aboard boat for transfer to ship.*

The Portuguese brought with them arquebuses, the first firearms to be seen in Japan. A contemporary Japanese described the clumsy weapon as an object two to three feet long, straight on the outside but with an inner passage. The inner passage, the record reads, runs through it but is closed at the end. At one side there is a hole—a passageway for fire. In use, the account continues, "it is filled with powder and lead pellets. Set up a small white target on a bank, grip the object in your hand, compose your body and, closing one eye, apply fire to the hole. The pellet hits the target squarely. The explosion is like lightning and the report like thunder. Bystanders must cover their ears. This thing with one blow can smash a mountain of silver and a wall of iron. If one sought to do mischief in another man's domain and he was touched by it, he would lose his life instantly."

Lords as well as commoners were intensely interested in this powerful new object. One lord, Tokitaka, spoke to the Portuguese leaders through an interpreter saying, "Incapable though I am, I should like to learn about it." Whereupon the Portuguese answered, "If you wish to learn about it, we shall teach you its mysteries." Lord Tokitaka then asked, "What is its secret?" The Portuguese replied, "The secret is to put your mind aright and close one eye." Lord Tokitaka answered, "The ancient sages have often taught how to set one's mind aright and I have learned something of it. If the mind is not set aright, there will be no logic for what we say or do. Thus, I understand what you say about

Barbary and Arabian horses were brought by the Portuguese. Priests and nobles watch horse race from the terrace.
◀ *Portuguese leaders confer with priests in front of Japanese teahouse. Materials for tea may be seen behind Portuguese.*

153

setting our minds aright. However, will it not impair our vision for objects at a distance if we close an eye? Why should we close an eye?" To which the foreigner replied, "That is because concentration is important in everything. When one concentrates, a broad vision is not necessary. To close an eye is not to dim one's eyesight but rather to project one's concentration farther. You should know this." Delighted, Lord Tokitaka said, "That corresponds to what Lao Tzu has said, 'Good sight means seeing what is very small'."

Later, Lord Tokitaka bought one of the firearms from the Portuguese and had the local iron workers make a copy of it. At first they were unsuccessful, but the Portuguese traders later taught the Japanese to make firearms in limited quantities and to train soldiers in their use. This account was written sixty years after the introduction of firearms. Guns, the writer observed, came to be called *tanegashima,* after the island where they first were seen.

Under a rich and decorated umbrella carried by slave, commander of Portuguese walks with officers and advisors.

The voyage from India to Japan was always hazardous, and the Portuguese lost many ships. But they continued to come. They were welcomed by a new leader, Oda Nobunaga, who had become the most powerful single force in Japan. It was his wish, he said, to "bring Japan under one sword." The guns introduced by the foreigners brought his wish closer to reality. The guns, together with his tenacity and a superbly trained army, were to give him supreme power over the country.

The Portuguese brought Christianity. Saint Francis Xavier, founder of the Society of Jesus, made the hazardous trip from Malacca in the company of a corsair named Yajiro whom he converted to Christianity, but who later returned to piracy. Asked if he were not afraid to make the trip through the treacherous waters infested with pirates, Saint Francis replied he feared neither shipwreck nor pirates but only the anger of God should he be remiss in his duties.

Landing at Satsuma, Saint Francis, following the Jesuit tradition of reaching the rulers as well as the common people, went directly to the

At top, Japanese and priest worship at a Christian altar. Below, Jesuits, Franciscans and merchants meet on roadway.

·P·FRĀCISCUSXAVERIVSSOCIEÆTISV

Portrait by Japanese artist of Saint Francis Xavier, founder of Society of Jesus, may be copy of a western painting.

local lord, who granted him permission to preach. There, during the next ten months, he brought the message of Christianity to peasants, warriors and lords. He argued theology with Buddhist monks and, although he did not succeed in converting any of them, he was successful in baptizing one hundred and fifty other Japanese.

This was only the beginning of the Jesuit success. Dedicated priests traveled across the country to the capital making converts along the way. They were fortunate in being in Kyoto when

Oda Nobunaga was in power.

Nobunaga was having trouble with armed Buddhist monks. He had burned down their great monastery at Mount Hiei and decapitated the inmates. Disliking Buddhists because they stood in the way of his political ambitions (except for one Zen sect), he welcomed the Christians. Nobunaga was no great believer in Japanese traditions and was receptive to exotic ideas. Believing that whatever the missionaries could teach him about foreign lands would be useful to

Most famous convert to Christianity was this lord of Bungo, baptized as Francisco in 1587. He is shown as a Buddhist.

him, he befriended them, and the devout but small company of Jesuits became regular visitors at his castle.

All was not easy for the Christian missionaries, for they were continuously opposed by Buddhist and Shintō priests, who pointed out to the populace that they were foreigners intent upon destroying and degrading the traditional gods of Japan. Yet they made progress. By the time Saint Francis returned to India saying, "These people are my delight," the missionaries were well established. Although many Japanese objected to Christian theology on the grounds that it unjustly condemned their ancestors to hell for the crime of not being previously exposed to Christianity, by 1571 there were 30,000 Japanese Christians. Ten years later, there were 150,000 and they were served by 200 churches, fifty-four priests and two seminaries. Even the lords of the virtually independent states of Bungo, Ōura and Arima were converted to Christianity, while in the capital itself at

Kyoto, high-ranking nobles and members of the military had embraced the Christian faith.

But the Portuguese brought more than guns and Christianity. They also brought the first Arabian horses which, when bred to the native Mongolian ponies, resulted in a larger, fleeter mount for the Japanese cavalry and nobility. They brought clocks, spectacles and thin, clear goblets. They taught the Japanese new techniques of weaving. At the end of the Muromachi period trade with Portugal had become a profitable enterprise for both Japanese and Portuguese. Christianity was becoming more firmly established with each passing year and Nobunaga, who had set out to bring all Japan under one sword, had, with fire-arms, almost succeeded

Portuguese priest with children who look Japanese and may be Christian converts.

MOMOYAMA PERIOD 1568-1600

Hideyoshi, one of Japan's greatest generals, continues the unification started by Nobunaga.... Though born a peasant, Hideyoshi puts an end to social mobility by prohibiting peasants from owning or carrying weapons or changing their occupations. He also prohibits military men from changing masters.... The gifts of Zen flourish—the tea ceremony, ink painting (*sumi-e*), garden designing and flower arranging.

HISTORICAL CHRONOLOGY		ART CHRONOLOGY	
1575	Nobunaga, using musketeers, defeated Takeda Katsuyori at Nagashino	c. 1570	Screen of maple viewing at Takao by Kanō Hideyori
1576	Nobunga moved to castle at Azuchi, near Kyoto	1576	Azuchi castle erected by Nobunaga; Kanō Eitoku made panel paintings for the castle
1582	Kyūshū Christian daimyo sent envoys to Rome; Nobunaga's death caused by Akechi Mitsuhide	c. 1580	Dog shooting screen
1585	Appointment of Hideyoshi as chancellor for Emperor Ōgimachi	1583	Portrait of Oda Nobunaga by Kanō Motohide
1586	Hideyoshi appointed prime minister of Emperor Go-Yōzei and given surname of Toyotomi	1583-5	Hideyoshi built Osaka castle
		1587	Juraku-tei (mansion of pleasures) erected by Hideyoshi
1587	Christian missionaries banned by Hideyoshi	c. 1587	Portrait of Ōtomo Sōrin
1590	Hideyoshi unified the country after the conquest of Odawara; Tokugawa Ieyasu installed in the Kanto provinces	1590	Kanō Eitoku died
		c. 1590	Popularity of pictures showing various professions
1592-3	First invasion of Korea		
1597	First persecution of Christians	1592-4	Fushimi castle erected for Hideyoshi
1597-8	Second invasion of Korea, ended at Hideyoshi's death	1598	Portrait of Hideyoshi
1600	Arrival of Will Adams on board the Dutch ship Liefde, subsequently made adviser to Ieyasu; victory of Ieyasu at the battle of Sekigahara	c. 1600	Namban byōbu (screens picturing westerners in Japan); western style paintings popular; scroll, Tawarakasane Kōsaku Emaki, showing rice farming

THE COUNTRY UNITED

The unification of Japan was brought about by two great general-heroes in the Momoyama period. The life of the first, Oda Nobunaga, was cut short as he was laying the foundation for single leadership over the entire country. He was succeeded in 1582 by Hideyoshi, perhaps Japan's greatest general, who was born into a peasant family and rose from a menial to prime minister and civil dictator.

While Nobunaga had succeeded in becoming leader over many of the independent lords, there was still much conflict among them, typified by the betrayal of Nobunaga himself by one of his trusted generals.

Many lords were defeated in battle by their own deputies, and the deputies in turn were destroyed by their vassals. Castle towns complete

Audience of wives, children and retainers watch traditional samurai sport called Inu Ou Mono *or the dog-chasing game.*
▶ *With mounted bowman in center, samurai prepare to release dog who must be shot before he escapes from circle.*

with customs barriers, private armies, knights and their military retainers fought among themselves.

Within the towns, members of guilds were allowed to sell their wares under the patronage of the ruling lord or of the church. It was a time when the guilds developed rapidly, and included workers in lacquer and brocades as well as scribes, fishermen and *sake* brewers. Many of the guilds, including the *sake* brewers, warehouse keepers and oil merchants, were protected by the large monasteries. In each case the artisans were taxed by their patrons.

To stabilize the situation Hideyoshi forbade peasants to own or carry arms. He prohibited agricultural workers from changing their profession and military men their masters. These new measures created a military caste and froze the status of tradesmen and peasants.

Ambitious beyond earlier rulers, Hideyoshi mounted an expedition to Korea and planned, in great detail, the conquest of China. Both projects failed, and he died while his troops were still in Korea.

Although Hideyoshi and Nobunaga were men of war, they were also, in the Japanese tradition, patrons and devotees of the arts. Both built magnificent castles and acted as patrons at the Imperial Court. Their castles, Azuchi, built by Nobunaga, and Osaka and Fushimi Castles on Momoyama (peach hill) near Kyoto built by Hideyoshi, were the grandest and most impregnable then known.

The regimes of Hideyoshi and Nobunaga saw the development and Japanization of the tea ceremony, ink painting (*sumi-e*), garden designing and flower arranging, all of them introduced by the Zen monks who studied in China.

◄ *Samurai carry a huge but light-weight replica of their shield in Kyoto's Gion festival which began in the ninth century.*
▼ *An official rides hurriedly on a mission. Gates could be barred against unwelcome intruders and were locked at night.*

JŌRURI, THE PUPPET THEATER

Realistic drama in the theater of Japan began with puppet plays. These were often religious in character and, in the early Momoyama period, performed within shrine or temple walls. The puppets, called *jōruri ningyō,* up to three-quarter life size, were manipulated with singing and

Enthusiastic audience inside puppet theater. Audience stands in front of small stage where puppets are manipulated.

instrumental accompaniment. The evolution of the puppet show was greatly enhanced by the introduction of the *samisen,* a mandolinlike instrument. The puppet shows included a visible puppet master and black-robed assistants. Gidayū, one of the great Genroku puppet masters, had a voice and style of such great distinction that a dramatic type of puppetry was named after him. The simple plots of the puppet plays often dealt with the valorous exploits of earlier warriors and the unrequited love they suffered at the hands of legendary heroines.

167

168

Street scene in early Kyoto shows fan shop and lacquer store. In roadway samurai quarrel, street vendors display wares.

169

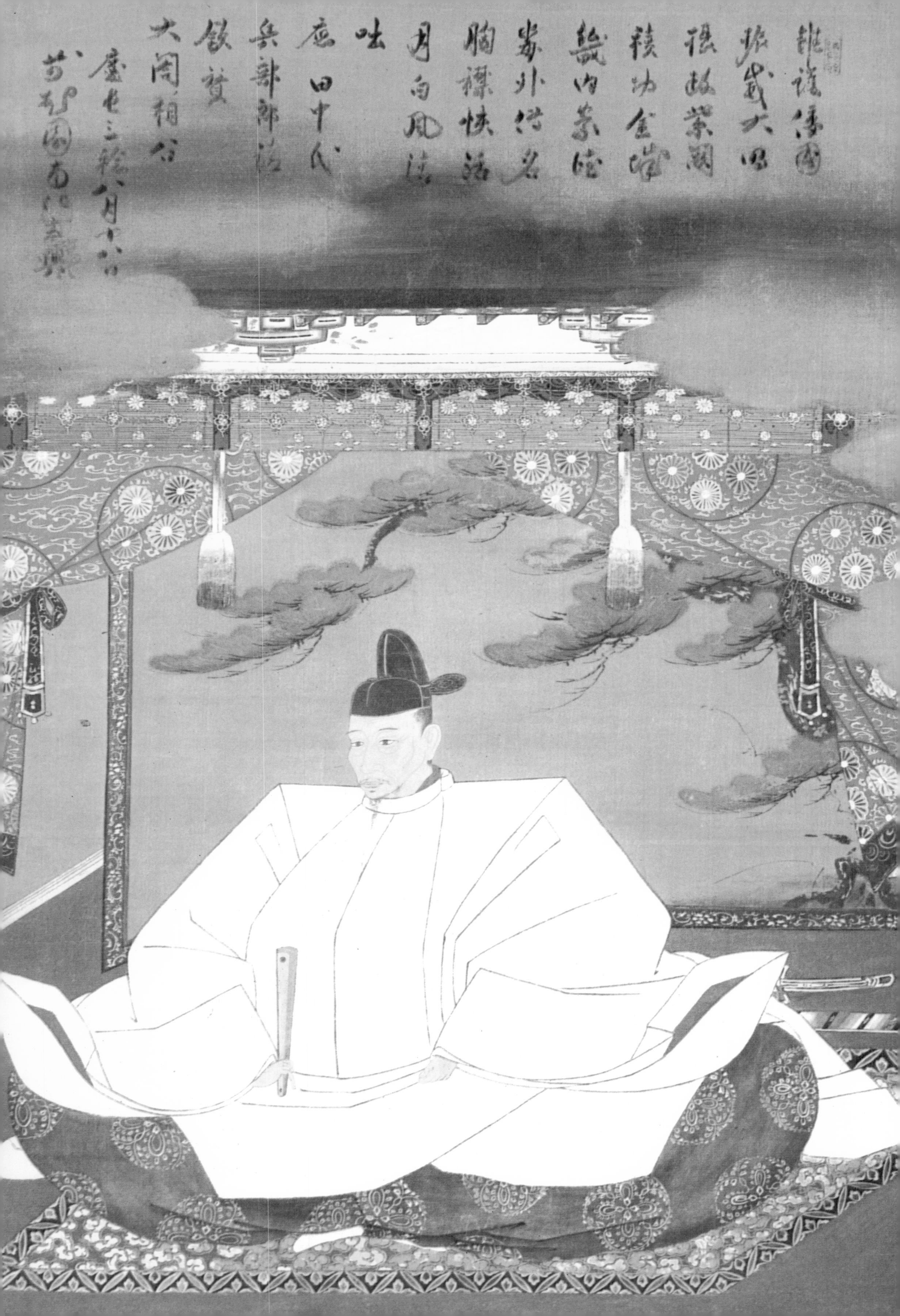

In his successful attempt to bring peace to various warring factions, the civil dictator, Hideyoshi, issued an edict which read in part, "People of the provinces are strictly forbidden to have in their possession any swords, short swords, bows, spears, firearms, or other types of arms." The edict added that the possession of weapons tended to cause uprisings and made the collection of taxes more difficult. The swords, it said, would be used as nails and bolts for the building of a great image of Buddha. All this, it pointed out, was being done to bring peace, security and happiness to the people; if people are in possession of agricultural implements only and devote themselves entirely to agriculture, they and their descendants will prosper.

While this measure did indeed bring peace and a certain stability to Japan, it also established the basis for a specific military caste system.

An edict issued three years later solidified the military caste by immobilizing other castes in the social system. This order forbade any peasant to abandon his fields either to take up trade or to become a laborer for hire. No military retainer was allowed to leave his master without permission, and no military man could change his status to work as an agriculturist or tradesman. The principle of collective responsibility, which meant that an entire village would be brought to justice should the law be evaded, became an important part of the legal code.

In spite of the strictness of these regulations, Hideyoshi was considered a generous and even a benevolent ruler in the modern political sense.

◄ *A commoner who rose to be a great hero, Toyotomi Hideyoshi combined great personal bravery and power diplomacy.*
▼ *In outdoor court of justice prisoner kneels while charges are read by advocate in center. Judge is seen upper left.*

Shadowy monkeys are shown in detail from sumi-e *screen.*
▼ *Japanese combination of* sumi-e *technique with realism is seen in screen showing farmer and ox resting at riverside.*

THE GIFTS OF ZEN

The pioneer Zen monk Eisai had brought tea from China along with the principles of Zen Buddhism four centuries earlier. During the Momoyama period the tea ceremony became a way of life.

Each part of the teahouse and each utensil within it had a purpose. The overhang of the roof above the entrance indicated the changeability of the weather and of human life. The gateway was low, so that the guest had to humble himself by stooping. Outside the house the steppingstones, the water basin and the stone lantern indicated a willingness to be used: the stones, to be trod upon; the water, to remove the dirt of the hands; the wick of the lantern, to be consumed that a little light might fall.

Within the house the faint incense satisfied the sense of smell. The sound of water being poured or boiling greeted the sense of hearing. The alcove with its single painting and simple flower arrangement pleased the sense of sight.

These impressions were repeated in the objects of the tea ceremony itself. The fire, the water, the spoon to measure the tea, the whisk to mix it, the plain iron kettle, the simple brown teapot and generous solid cups, all did their part aesthetically and realistically.

Zen priests had also introduced ink painting called *sumi-e,* which has been described as painting by spontaneous inspiration. The paper is fragile, the brush coarse, and each line made must be final. There is no overpainting, no building up, no planning of the image. It is an attempt to project inner meaning through direct, broad strokes. Among the great painters in this style was Hasegawa Tōhaku, who adapted the Chinese Zen-inspired technique to Japanese themes.

Famous sumi-e *painting shows hermit brothers who gave* up *their riches to live a life of poverty and contemplation.*

THE WAY OF THE GODS

The Ise shrine, earliest Shintō place of worship in Japan, was built to the Sun Goddess, who was considered the ancestor of the Imperial Family, and became the symbol of fertility and prosperity to the nation. Like all Shintō shrines, it is entered through a gateway called *torii*. Close at hand is a basin where the mouth and the hands may be washed. This custom, *misogi,* the washing of the body, is symbolic of spiritual cleanliness, as the ritual of purification (*harai*) of the room is symbolic of the elimination of evil spirits.

At Ise, two deities are enshrined. The Sun Goddess is the object of worship in the inner shrine. The deity which represents fertility and national prosperity is located in the outer shrine. In every shrine a symbolic mirror is placed.

The Sun Goddess instructed her grandchild to illuminate the world with light like the mirror, to reign over the world with the jewel, and to sub-

due those who will not obey with the divine sword. It has been said that the mirror has the form of the sun, the jewel the moon, and the sword the substance of the stars.

The inner precinct of the Ise shrine was the only Shintō holy place which was never open to Buddhist monks. It was the exception that proved the general trend of religious life up through the Momoyama period, which was toward a blending of eastern religious beliefs.

The tradition of early Japanese rulers worshiping in both Buddhist temples and Shintō shrines was typified by the death of Hideyoshi, who had written: "God is the root and source of all existence. This God is spoken of by Buddhism in India, Confucianism in China and Shintō in Japan. To know Shintō is to know Buddhism as well as Confucianism." At his death, a Shintō shrine was raised to his memory above the great Buddha image he had erected.

◄ *At entrance to inner Ise shrine, most sacred of all Shintō temples, commoners take ritual cleansing bath in Isuzu River.*
► *Outer Ise shrine is dedicated to the prosperity of the nation. Small red walled building enshrines the god of fertility.*

High-born lady of samurai class holds a Buddhist juzu while chanting prayers. Painting is fine example of Momoyama art.

EDO-TOKUGAWA PERIOD 1600-1853

Early trade expansion is followed by closing of country.... Christians persecuted and expelled.... Isolation from the world brings peace and a thriving culture at home. ...The Kabuki Theatre, *haiku* poetry, "floating world" pictures *(ukiyo-e)*.... The Tokugawa rule effectively, but prosperity eludes the nation.... The slight opening to the West, a Dutch trading post, allows the infiltration of ideas that stir the imagination of young Japanese.

HISTORICAL CHRONOLOGY		ART CHRONOLOGY	
1603	*Ieyasu assumed title of Shōgun at Edo*	1602-3	*Nijō castle built by Ieyasu*
c. 1603	*Early* Kabuki *with women performers*	1605-15	*Screens and scrolls of early* Kabuki
1609	*Dutch factory established at Hirado*	1616	*Ieyasu's portrait painted*
1614-5	*Battles of Osaka; Ieyasu victorious*	1617	*Kanō Tanyū employed as painter to the Shōgun; construction of the Nikkō Tō-shōgū (Tokugawa mausoleum) begun*
1616	*Death of Ieyasu*		
1636	*Ban on Japanese travel abroad*	1688-1704	*Genroku period; during this time* ukiyo-e *(floating world) art popular*
1638	*Portuguese traders forced to leave Japan*		
1641	*Dutch traders transferred from Hirado to Deshima*	c. 1700	*Gold screen of iris by Kōrin*
		1765	*Beginning of* nishiki-e *(brocade picture) i.e. true polychrome print by Harunobu*
1657	*Great fire of Edo; compilation of Daini-honshi (History of Japan) begun*	c. 1780	*Sado gold mine scroll*
1694	*Bashō,* haiku *poet, died*	1780	*View of Hollanders' factory in Deshima print*
1720	*Relaxation of ban on importation of western books*	1793	*Utamaro's prints of famous beauties*
1774	*First Japanese translation of Dutch book*	1794	*Prints of actors by Sharaku*
1804	*Arrival of Rezanov, Russian envoy*	1817	*Picture of the Blomhoff family by Kawahara Keiga*
1825-42	*Exclusionist policy reinforced*	1829	*Katsushika Hokusai published his "Thir-ty-six Views of Mount Fuji" (Fugaku Sanjūrokukei)*
1837	*Rice riots in Osaka; U.S. ship,* Morrison, *visited Edo Bay*		
1853	*Arrival of Commodore Matthew C. Perry at Uraga*	1833	*Andō Hiroshige published series "Fifty-three Stages on the Tōkaidō (eastern sea highway)"*

ISOLATION AND PROGRESS

The Tokugawa Shōgunate ruled Japan effectively and peacefully for 265 years. It turned away from foreign adventures and, except for a brief period at the beginning, kept foreigners and foreign influence out of Japan, using the time of long isolation for internal consolidation.

The Shōgunate was founded by Tokugawa Ieyasu in 1603. Having come to power through military conquest, the Shōgun rewarded his supporters with extensions of their domains. But enemies were treated with consideration and allowed to occupy less productive areas in remote

Stone for castle wall is carried on cart while workers help bullocks to move the load. Boy atop stone sings folk song.

regions; they were known as the outer lords.

The central government divided the country among some 250 feudal lords, and each of them was required to spend a portion of the year at Edo, the new capital, which later became Tokyo. To reduce the possibility of conspiracy, all lords were forced to leave their families as hostages throughout the year.

The Emperor and his court were allocated adequate revenues and the Tokugawas never sought the throne for themselves. But the Emperor's functions were confined to traditional,

ceremonial and religious leadership. To discourage any attempt at Imperial restoration, a Tokugawa garrison was maintained near the Imperial headquarters. No vassal was allowed to approach the Emperor except through a Tokugawa intermediary.

The lords were generally free to operate their fiefs without interference so long as they remained loyal to the Shōgun. The edicts forbidding nonmilitary classes from carrying arms were continued from the Momoyama period, as were the laws prohibiting change of occupation.

While Buddhism continued to be influential, Confucianism, with its emphasis on ethical conduct, made strides among the scholars, the intellectual leaders and even the samurai warriors.

Indeed, the samurai used this extended time of peace to add intellectual attainments to the exercise of military skills. The famous code of *bushidō*, "the way of the warrior," combining Confucian morality with traditional bravery and loyalty, was designed to stress responsibility of the samurai to his Emperor and the state.

The fate of the Christian converts, however, was anything but peaceful. Continuous persecutions were the rule and after a Christian-led peasant rebellion in 1637, Christianity was completely eradicated. The Portuguese and Spanish were banished.

However, a window was left open to the West. A tiny enclave of Dutch traders was allowed to occupy an outpost at Deshima in Nagasaki har-

bor and to carry on limited trade with carefully licensed Japanese. Through this opening came a slow trickle of western knowledge.

As peace continued through the eighteenth century the status of the merchant class improved, and a renaissance in literature, the theater and the arts spread from the capital to the country. There was time to cultivate the Japanese love of elegance and outward enjoyment of living. Isolation, instead of stifling the arts, gave it an impetus. There was a considerable increase in the number of volumes printed and read in Japan. Early newspapers printed from tile blocks gave accounts of battles and natural disasters. These were soon followed by the extensive development of wood-block prints and gave rise to genre painting which recorded in detail the life of people on all social levels.

But as the new culture expanded, there was a continuing regard for the early art of the country which was rarely equalled by the new.

During the final years of isolation, the Russians, Americans, British, and French knocked impatiently on the closed door. Within the nation there were stirrings of scholars and intellectuals. The little that had trickled in through the open window at Nagasaki had created a thirst for more knowledge of the world, and a highly developed civilization was ready to receive it.

◄ *Ieyasu rebuilt this castle in Edo in the seventeenth century. Feudal lord approaches castle followed by samurai.*
▼ *One of many stations on the Tōkaidō Road to control traffic to and from capital. Small teahouse awaits travelers.*

IEYASU

After fighting through the bloody wars that rocked Japan at the end of the sixteenth century and seeing the effects of Japan's defeat in its attempt to invade Korea and China, the new Shōgun, Tokugawa Ieyasu, was determined to follow a course of peace and unity. A heavy man, short and sturdy, he lived most of his life on horseback. Ieyasu was nevertheless intensely interested in books. He once said, "If we cannot clarify the principle of human relations, society and government will become unstable and disorders will never cease. Books are the only means whereby these principles can be set forth and understood."

Ieyasu adopted a Confucian code of ethics although he remained a devout Buddhist throughout his life and expanded his beliefs to include the native deities of Shintō, whom he regarded as manifestations of the Buddha. Confucian philosophy served him well, for his first interest was an orderly country under the direction of an orderly government.

Unlike Hideyoshi, his predecessor, or Hide-tada, his successor, Ieyasu did not enforce the edicts against Christianity with vigor. For a short time during his regime, more Christians actually infiltrated Japan and certain churches were rebuilt. In a discussion with his ministers, he remarked that one maxim had served him well: "Requite malice with kindness."

Enthusiastic about foreign trade which flourished during his regime, he was reluctant to take measures to isolate the country. Most of the edicts closing off foreign trade and forbidding Japanese to travel abroad were promulgated after his death.

During the latter years of Ieyasu's life, he retired to Shizuoka Castle at Suruga. Always an outdoor man, he said he loved Suruga because of the magnificent view of Fuji and the opportunity for good hunting.

Upon his death, one of the greatest Shintō shrines in all Japan was raised in his memory, the Tōshōgū at Nikkō. It was dedicated to him as architect of Japan's most lasting peace, the Buddha incarnate, the Sun God of the East.

▶ *Tokugawa Ieyasu, founder of Tokugawa Shōgunate, unified the country and brought peace after the death of Hideyoshi.*

THE COUNTRY OPEN

In the earliest years of the Tokugawa Shōgunate, Japanese ships carrying vermillion stamped trading permits traveled freely throughout Asia making trips to Macao, Luzon, and innumerable Chinese ports.

As soon as Korea had recovered from the unsuccessful invasion by the Japanese, trade was reopened with that country. Three hundred Korean envoys were royally feted as they traveled from station to station up the Tōkaidō Road.

Chinese and Portuguese traders were welcomed. From the Portuguese the Japanese

learned all they could of mapmaking and navigation. These excellent sailors also acted as pilots on Japanese ships.

Ieyasu, the first Tokugawa Shōgun, made friends with a young and ingenious Englishman, Will Adams, who landed in Japan in the year 1600. Adams, a pilot and gunner, became a trusted aide to Ieyasu and did much to improve the budding Japanese navy. Adams later wrote that the Japanese were good by nature, courteous beyond measure and valiant in war.

Confucian ethics, which dominated trade, confirmed the good opinion held by Adams. Ship owners and crews were required to swear an oath that they would abide by a policy of fair dealing that forbade excess profit taking and exploiting differences in nationality and that enjoined equal treatment for all and a respectful attitude toward the traditions of other countries.

There were some disadvantages to foreign trade of which the Tokugawa Shōgunate was conscious. Piracy was rife throughout the Asian waters. Smuggling was commonplace, and during this period many Christians entered the country illegally. Slowly distrust of Christian motives developed into an overwhelming fear of domination by the Spanish and the Portuguese.

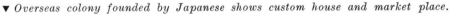

◄ *Before the closing of Japan to foreigners, small ships, such as this one, traded with many Asian countries. Portuguese pilots were employed whenever available.*
▼ *Overseas colony founded by Japanese shows custom house and market place.*

THE COUNTRY CLOSED

The thought, said to have been expressed by a Spanish trader, that Christianity was a springboard for military expansion and domination, may have contributed to the expulsion of the Spanish and the Portuguese from Japan. Christianity at this time was militant throughout the Spanish and Portuguese colonies, and Japanese converts may have exhibited political tendencies at home. Certainly suppression and even martyrdom did not affect their ardor. Between 1613 and 1626, it is estimated by the Church, 3,125 Japanese Christians suffered martyrdom at the hands of the government rather than give up their faith. An indication of how strong was the fear of dominance by the Christians was the oath required of Japanese who renounced Chistianity. It included a section confessing that the Christian Church could do what it liked with its people by threatening excommunication and hellfire, and that it was really a plot to take over the countries of others.

Climax of the suppression of Christianity came when 37,000 Christian-led peasants rebelled in Shimabara. The Shōgunate acted quickly. The resulting battle became a massacre. This was the end of Christianity in feudal Japan.

Early restrictions isolating the country decreed death to the crews of Portuguese or Spanish ships touching on Japan. Edicts followed prohibiting all foreign travel by Japanese under penalty of death. The building of ships large enough to engage in foreign trade was prohibited. In addition to the Spanish and Portuguese, English and Russians were excluded. Only a few Dutch and Chinese traders were allowed to remain. Foreign books were forbidden.

A choice, it was felt, had to be made between the assurance of internal peace and unity by closing the country or inviting dissension and unrest through intercourse with foreign nations. The Tokugawa Shōgunate chose isolation.

◀ *Nobles fishing with cormorants. The birds have a cord around their necks, preventing them from swallowing the fish.*
▼ *Working as a team, intrepid fishermen snare whale in net, then throw harpoons. Banners indicate whale has been caught.*

Three recently caught whales are being processed by swarms of busy villagers. According to a Japanese proverb, when one

whale is caught it makes seven villages prosperous. On right a winch is being used to pull a whale jaw across the beach.

THE NEW ECONOMY

As the cities of feudal Japan grew, conflict arose between the rice economy of the country and the money economy of the towns which developed with the growth of the merchant class.

These tradesmen were taxed unmercifully. Nevertheless, they prospered. Some were permitted to improve wasteland by the Shōgunate. This was only one of the many breaks in the feudal wall. Uprisings of peasants, caused by the unequal distribution of wealth, and minor revolts against individual lords were other straws in the wind.

The position of the samurai, and there were a great many of them, became especially difficult. He was a warrior without a war. Because he had been elevated to a high social status, he tried to maintain the appearance of prosperity. But his pay was small, and he was forced to look elsewhere for an income. The Shōguns and feudal

190

lords gave what help they could. They declared moratoriums on samurai loans, but at the same time they sometimes were forced to reduce stipends to their loyal retainers. These measures were not effectual. But many samurai showed unexpected resourcefulness. They became students, writers, artists, teachers and politicians. Some, to survive, became innkeepers, artisans and agricultural workers.

The Tokugawa government, with a growing need for more money to support an increasing standard of living, began to move toward a centralized, and away from a feudal, structure. In spite of occasional localized riots, no attempt by the masses to change the government was possible. But the students, merchants, emerging bankers and young intellectual leaders could. Toward the end of the Tokugawa regime, the Shōgunate issued a wave of new edicts, including censorship, abolition of guilds, recoinage of money and new tax levies on tradesmen. But they did not stick. There seemed to be a growing awareness, even within the government, of the necessity for change. It came with the arrival of Commodore Matthew C. Perry.

◄ *Gold being washed at Shōgunate mine on Sado Island, Japan Sea. Gold was discovered by the mid-eighth century.*
▼ *Gold ingots being reduced for marking. At right, coins called Ō-ban and Ko-ban, are being stamped and weighed.*

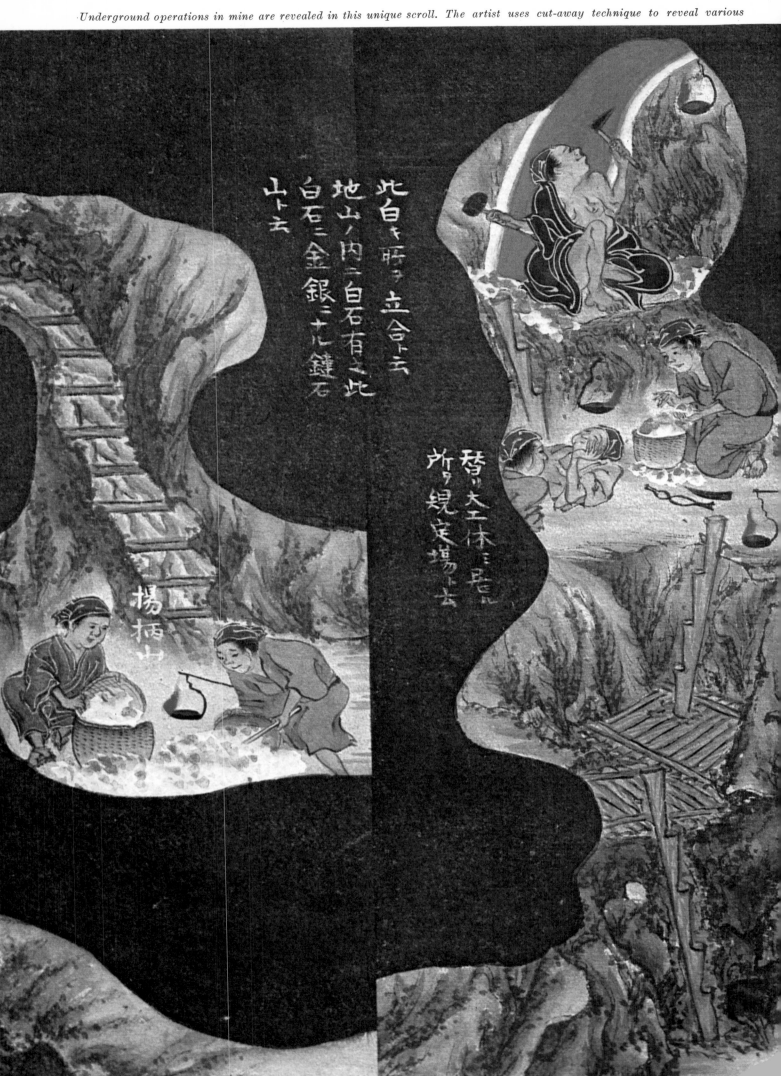

underground operations. White silver-bearing ore is being removed from the mine in buckets shown at far right.

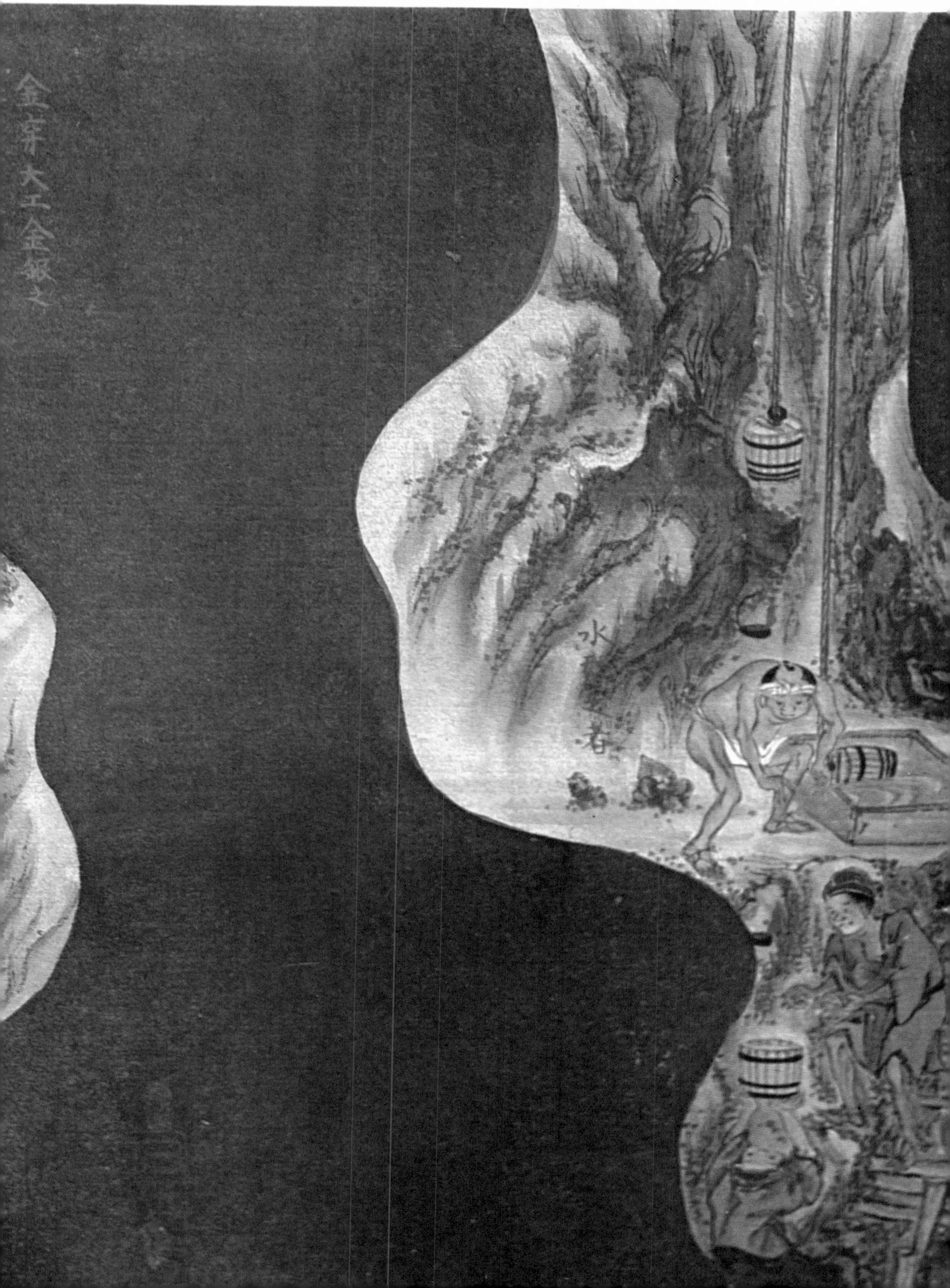

THE DUTCH INFLUENCE

The western influence in Japan that was later to have a distinct effect upon the weakening of the feudal Tokugawa government began before that government was formed. Two men—an Englishman, Will Adams, and a Dutchman, Jan Joostan van Loderstein—were shipwrecked along the Japanese coast. Both found favor with Tokugawa Ieyasu, who was then coming to power.

When members of the Dutch East India Company sailed into Japan, Ieyasu let them set up a trading post. He suggested Uraga, near the capital at Edo (Tokyo). But the Dutch preferred to be far away from the center of government and settled at Hirado near Nagasaki.

The Dutch built sturdy square stone warehouses and living quarters in contrast to the delicate wood structures of local citizenry. On the edge of the harbor they constructed the first lighthouse in Japan, a stone tower where fires could be lighted to guide their ships into the settlement.

Traders from China, Korea and even from the British East India Company visited Hirado, but it was not destined to become a permanent trad-

194

▲ *Close-up of the Dutch settlement at Nagasaki. Prominent details are ship in harbor, flagpole, large building, and jetty.*

◄ *An elephant, imported by Dutch merchants as a gift to the Shōgun, was not accepted. First example of ukiyo-e showing a foreigner.*

ing colony. Difficulties arose first with the Spanish and then with the Portuguese, who were banished ostensibly for their efforts to spread Christianity. After the edict closing the country, the Dutch, along with some Chinese and Korean traders, were moved to an island off the coast of Nagasaki called Deshima.

The British returned to Japan more than 150 years later, when they were at war with Holland. Two British ships, *Charlotte* and *Maria,* entered Nagasaki harbor, but a strong Dutch leader, Hendrick Doeff, refused to surrender Dutch trade rights to the British. As a result of this visit by the British and another threat in 1824, the Shōgunate ordered all foreign ships driven off (*uchiharai*). The death penalty was usually meted out to the crews.

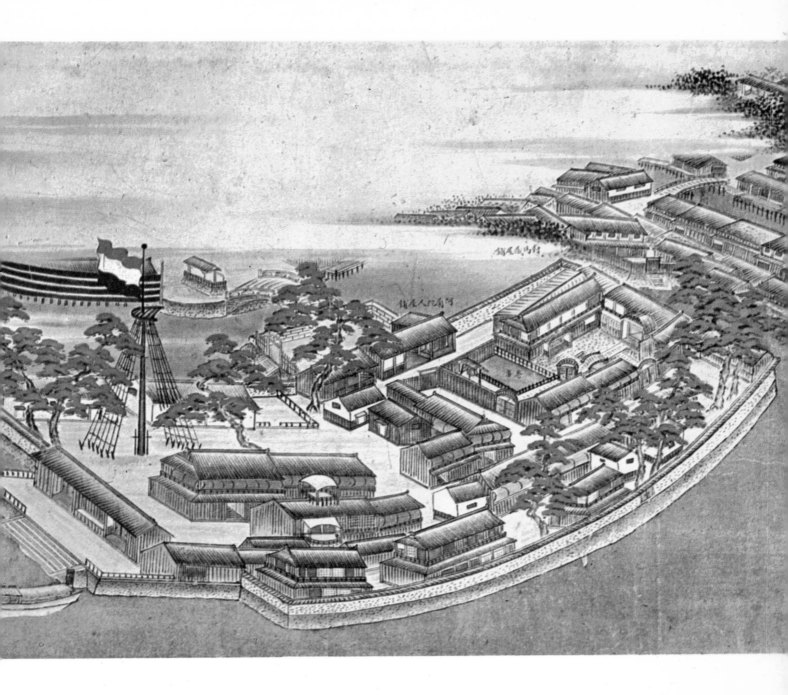

Young Japanese, curious about the West, began to reach out for new knowledge. Their story is a highly dramatic one that begins when interpreter-students learned to read forbidden Dutch works. During the early days of the Tokugawa Shōgunate all foreign books had been banned, but this edict was raised in 1720 on books that were not concerned with Christianity. The first students to take up Dutch had an extraordinarily difficult time, first laboriously learning the language, then struggling with the problem of fitting western ideas into Japanese language and thought patterns. Books were passed surreptitiously from scholar to scholar, and often entire volumes were copied by hand. Even after the ban on foreign books was lifted by the Shōgun Yoshimune, students faced major problems in their attempts to adapt western scientific knowledge to Japanese use.

Their first efforts were put into the study of mathematics and navigation. Some scholars felt that knowledge of navigation and astronomy was essential for Japan's future. By the middle period of the Tokugawa Shōgunate a conviction was spreading that if the country was to progress it had to break out of isolation. Such ideas were contagious, and the small group of *rangakusha*, Dutch scholars, grew in knowledge and in influence. In 1774, the first book on European ideas written by a Japanese was printed in Japan. Other books followed—on military and naval matters, medicine (the students once dissected the corpse of a criminal by following the illustrations in a Dutch book) (*Continued on page* 200)

▲ Gaily dressed Dutch dine while children play in street below. Turkey and young bull were imported. Dutch brought servants from Southeast Asia.
◄ Billiard game is in progress at Dutch settlement. Japanese artist used modified bird's-eye-view technique in order to illustrate house interiors.
► Portrait of a resident manager at the Deshima trading post. This picture is portion of unique collection owned by Japanese Kobe Museum.

▼ *Violating rule against European women in the Dutch colony, Jan Blomhoff arrived with his family. They were expelled.*
▶ *Pensive Japanese girl and Dutchman on the waterfront. Only women allowed in colony were geishas and prostitutes.*

De Opregte Afteekening van het Opper hoofd Jacock Blomhoff, Zijn Vrouw en Kind, die in Aᵒ 1818 al hier aan gekomen zijn.

(*Continued from page* 197) and geography.

The growing fund of knowledge gleaned from the Dutch was only a very small part of the scholarship extant in Japan. Young samurai and religious scholars, after studying their own history and that of England and China, were also looking forward to the time when Japan would play an important role in international affairs.

The Dutch traders at Deshima led the same kind of life as they enjoyed in Holland. Tables, chairs, beds and kitchen utensils were imported for their quarters. Even billiard tables were imported in an attempt to make life pleasant.

Their greatest hardship was isolation. The man-made island of Deshima, constructed in Nagasaki harbor under the direction of the Shōgunate, was designed deliberately to keep them from contact with the Japanese people. The authorities wanted, among other things, to prevent the fathering of children of mixed blood. Yet the Japanese adamantly refused to allow the traders to send for their wives from Holland. When one Dutch administrator, Jan Cock Blomhoff, brought his wife, children and their nurse, they were promptly deported.

The Japanese seemed to have been fortunate in the type of men selected to direct the Dutch merchants. Dr. Engelbert Kaempfer was an author as well as a doctor. Isaac Titsingh, who headed the post in 1779, was a distinguished scholar and diplomat. Dutch scientific knowledge went into the building of boats and forts, and the casting of cannon by the Saga domain. A foundry and gun smithy were constructed by the Japanese from Dutch models.

When Japan finally opened its doors to the West, it was the Dutch traders and the Japanese scholars who had learned so much from them who paved the way for a comparatively smooth transition to a modern state.

鳥居清倍筆

THE
FLOATING
WORLD

There is a Japanese word that means many things to many people. It is *ukiyo*. Its origin is uncertain. Most Japanese think of it as a way of life, while most Europeans think of it as a woodblock print. It means both, for the work of the artists of this period became known throughout the world as *ukiyo-e*, "floating world pictures."

Once it had a sad connotation. The implication of the word *uki*, "floating" changed, however, from "transient," or "impermanent" and therefore sad, to "lively" and "gay" and with this came a connection with the gay life of the time.

This turnabout occurred near the end of the seventeenth century, which also saw a new type

of literature based on the novels of Saikaku, a new form and content in poetry, *haiku,* developed to a fine art by Bashō, and an evolution in the *Kabuki* theater from simple dance performances to dramatic plays. This renaissance in the arts, called the Genroku period, even brought new and colorful designs to household decoration and clothing.

Much of this resulted from a gradual increase in educational materials. Popular authors and talented artists brought books within reach of an ever-increasing audience. The arts were removed from the exclusive province of the nobility and spread over the countryside.

四
季
大
ゆ
り

Kabuki *theater before women were forbidden to appear. The orchestra is seated above. Woman nurses baby at lower right.*

KABUKI

From the austerity and understatement of the religion-oriented Nō plays and the romantic dramas of the *jōruri* puppet theater came the highly realistic form of theater called *Kabuki*. It soon became the most important form of entertainment in Tokugawa Japan. Elaborate and romantic dramas were enacted on huge stages. Movable scenery, special lighting effects and ingenious use of theatrical illusion made possible the staging of fires, hurricanes and snowstorms with telling effect on the audience.

Kabuki plays included dramatic incident, music and dance. Costuming was always fresh and brilliant. Female performers were forbidden entirely in 1629, and the government later proclaimed that only adult men known as *onnagata* (female impersonators) should play women's parts. Actors developed large followings and every Edoite had his favorite. Artists sold thousands of theatrical portraits.

Plays became more complex and acting more subtle in the *Kabuki* theater during the Genroku era at the end of the seventeenth century. Most plays, however, still dealt with heroes, loyalty and tragedy. Perhaps the most successful and most frequently performed of all *Kabuki* plays was the story of the forty-seven *rōnin*. It tells of a lord who, after being insulted, draws his sword and wounds his foe. In this peaceful period, it was a capital crime for a sword to be drawn within the confines of the Shōgun's walls.

Kabuki *actors apply make-up and don costumes for performance of heroic drama. Their dressing room is portable.*

Eighteenth century Kabuki *drama about vendetta by two brothers. Artist shows strong western influence.* ▼ *Three* sumō *wrestlers wear the traditional* mawashi *(fringed half-skirt). Calligraphy gives names of champions.*

The unhappy man is forced to commit formal suicide, but the instigator of the affair, Lord Kira, goes free.

Forty-seven of the deceased's retainers, now masterless men called *rōnin*, swear to avenge their lord's death by killing Lord Kira. The suspense builds as they plan their revenge. One winter morning (with dramatic snowfall effect) they gain entry into Lord Kira's villa, cut off his head and take it to their master's tomb. Dramatically, after making peace with the dead, they commit themselves to the Shōgunate for justice. Now the plot becomes purely Japanese. Two arguments are advanced: 1) that they should be pardoned and 2) that only a sentence of honorable suicide would satisfy the law and also the unspoken wishes of the loyal *rōnin*. Having avenged their lord, it is argued, they would want to join him in the world beyond. The latter argument seems proper to the Shōgun, and all of the *rōnin* commit mass *seppuku*.

▶ *Portrait of famous female impersonator,* onnagata, *is one of series by Sharaku whose career lasted one year.*

CHERRY BLOSSOMS AND MAPLE LEAVES

The pleasures of cherry blossom viewing and picnics during the clear spring weather have always been an important part of Japanese living. Paintings of cherry blossoms and maple leaves date back to the mid-Heian period.

Throughout the country, from late March to early May, fifty varieties of cherry trees burst into bloom. It is the signal for hundreds of thousands of Japanese to pack hampers of food and don spring kimonos to go forth and greet these harbingers of summer.

The peasant sage Ninomiya wrote:

The well-trod path
Is covered with fallen leaves
Sweep them aside
To view the footprints of the Sun Goddess.

◄ *A picnic party in cherry blossom time. This group carries a lunch box and a musical instrument called* samisen. ▼ *Setting out on a holiday, family carries food hampers and* sake *jug. Rice paddies on right lead to Shintō shrine.*

In 1750 Fujiwara Mitsutaka of the Tosa school painted a detailed screen showing life in Kyoto. In this detail from the

212

ARTS AND ARTISANS

The work of the artisans of Japan was well recorded by artists from the tenth through the nineteenth centuries. But the most sensitive record of craftsmen practicing their trades was left by Hokusai, the last great master of *ukiyo-e*-style painting, who died in 1849. Throughout his long life, which stretched eighty-nine years, he made sketches with amazing facility of the common people of Japan, as they went about their daily tasks. His painting was by no means limited to artisans at work. He also revealed the joys and sorrows, poverty and affluence, realism and fantasy in the lives of his subjects.

During the years that Hokusai painted artisans, strong guilds called *kumiai* had developed. These groups of craftsmen banded together to stabilize prices. The number of members of a guild was strictly limited and so was the number of apprentices that each master craftsman was allowed. Many of the guilds were under the protection of a powerful patron. The makers of *sake* had as their protector the Kitano Shintō shrine. The Gion shrine in Kyoto exercised control over the workers in cotton. Other groups had as their patrons powerful *daiymo* or long-established Buddhist temples.

Even with the considerable control that existed, the artisan of Japan was able to produce his wares on a highly individual basis. He was the creator, craftsman, manufacturer and usually the seller of his products. Often an artisan working with his family or apprentices would process the raw silk or cotton, weave it, design and dye it, and offer it for sale.

◄ *Women prepare cotton for spinning, using a tool called* kinuta. *Man at right carries bundles of refined cotton fiber.*
▼ *Using indigo two men put design on cloth in this detail from a six-fold screen on country occupations by Hokusai.*

Hunting reached its peak in the Edo-Tokugawa period. At left, beaters drive deer, boars and rabbits into an en-

closure. On the right, the animals are met by hunters. Note how far back lines extend to prevent animals from escaping.

215

Two women in intimate kitchen scene by the famous artist Utamaro. One peels vegetables while other cares for baby.

Companion print shows fire making. Girl in foreground blows coals. The other, getting smoke in her eyes, uses ladle.

BIRTH OF
THE METROPOLIS

Around a small fortress in east Japan a small village was established. Like Rome, it had seven hills. Between and surrounding them were desolate lowlands and marshes. From 1457 until the end of the sixteenth century it remained a quiet agricultural and fishing hamlet. Then Tokugawa Ieyasu received it from Hideyoshi; it was part of the eight provinces of the Kantō region that Ieyasu won as a reward in battle. The town was called Edo and Ieyasu made it his capital of Japan in 1603. It was later renamed Tokyo (eastern capital).

When the Shōgun moved to the new capital with his thousands of retainers, he was followed by artisans, tradesmen and servants to supply the needs of the affluent ruling class. Builders and carpenters were imported by the hundreds to construct homes for the 250 feudal lords ordered by the Shōgun to keep their families in Edo as hostages.

An extensive area known as Yoshiwara ("nightless city") was set aside where licensed courtesans entertained wealthy merchants, artists, artisans and writers.

Almost overnight the village became a city. Bridges spanned the many creeks and rivers, and over them moved an unending stream of humanity. Within the first hundred years, Edo reached a population of half a million and by 1787 it had increased to 1,367,900. It was well on its way to becoming the world's largest city.

Bird's-eye view of city of Edo, later to be named Tokyo, shows rivers, bridges, Chiyoda castle on right and Mt. Fuji.

▶ *Japan's greatest city was destroyed by fire many times. Here firemen place white standards to show center of fire.*
▼ *Fireworks show on river Sumida in Edo. It is probable that fireworks caused some of the devastating fires.*

THE FIRE FIGHTERS OF EDO

Fire fighting was an important part of the daily life of most men of Edo. By the year 1858 they lived in a city as big as London with houses built entirely of wood and paper. Oil lanterns were in use throughout the city; cooking was done on open charcoal braziers (*hibachi*), and fireworks were a regular entertainment. This incendiary combination gave rise to devastating fires.

Every block had its fire-fighting company. Each company carried its own standard, a distinctive cloth decoration on a long pole. Membership in a brigade was handed down from father to son.

When a fire started, the signal was given by a fire watcher, who climbed a ladder to strike the fire gong. Firemen raced to the scene of the conflagration. Upon reaching the blaze, the man carrying the standard climbed as near as possible to the center of the flames and directed the efforts of their company. The standard identified each brigade, so they could be rewarded later. In spite of the energy and bravery of the firemen, the annual loss by fire in Edo was staggering. Every merchant put money aside each year for rebuilding, knowing someday he would be burned out.

220

Famous restaurant Kawachiro was located at present Ueno Park. Scene shows geishas from gay quarters entertaining diners.
▶ *Exterior of Echigoya Drapers Shop, an Edo landmark. It was the predecessor of the great Mitsukoshi Department Store.*
▼ *The interior of the Echigoya shop shows customers' shoes on floor, clerks and customers seated on tatami mats.*

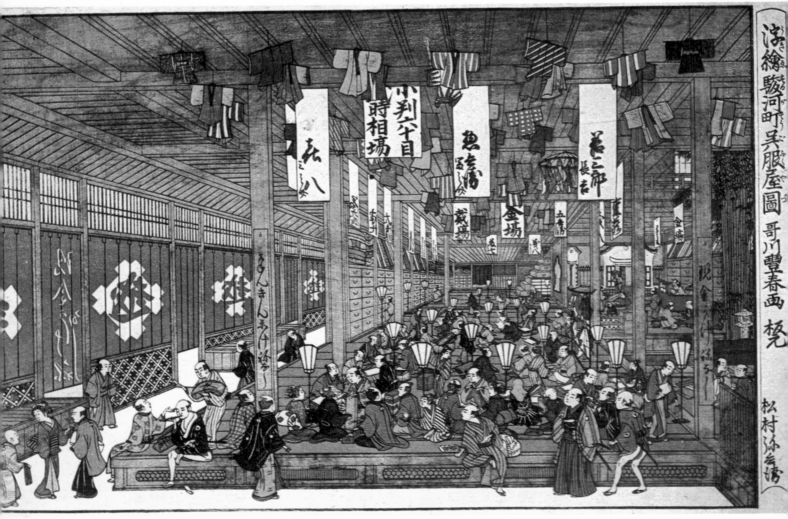

SHOPS AND SHOPPING

Beside temples and shrines long arcades of shops developed. Most were little more than stalls from six to ten feet wide and perhaps ten to fifteen feet deep. The fronts were open to the street and allowed every passerby a full view of articles for sale and the craftsmen. As the city of Edo prospered, it became the shopping center of Japan, and certain regions became known for special kinds of articles. Some streets were devoted largely to selling decorations and paper goods, others to religious articles. Some specialized in books, others were bright with the color of wood-block prints. But in the fast-growing Ginza (a word which originally meant "mint", for early coins were stamped in this section), shops of every type were jumbled together. Shops selling umbrellas, sandals and clogs, kimono, lanterns, fans and seals lined both sides of the wide roadway.

Merchants became prosperous during the Edo period, for the families of the rich *daimyo* were held as hostages and did all of their shopping within the city. Due to the patronage of this rich clientele, larger and more exclusive stores developed. Some like Echigoya Drapers Shop, a favorite of the elite, were to become the great department stores of the future.

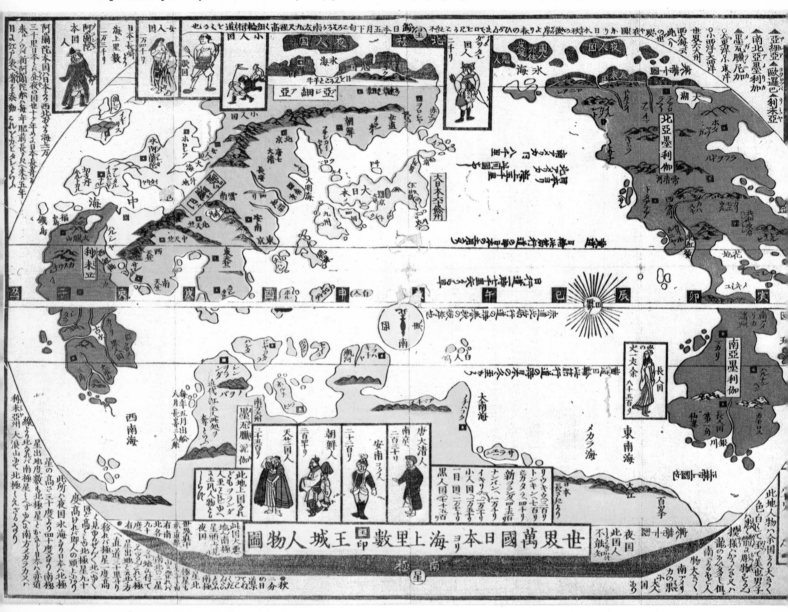

THE JAPANESE WORLD

The 265 years of isolation had a predictable effect upon Japan's lack of knowledge of the outside world. Before the country was closed, a few scholars and seamen had learned something about the size and shape of the world from the Portuguese. But the Portuguese were expelled by 1638, and the great mass of the Japanese people learned little of geography from the isolated enclave of Dutchmen. The earliest maps of Japan mirrored the distorted view of the world as interpreted by seventeenth century cartographers working from limited Portuguese knowledge. Later maps, although more realistic, indicated countries of one-eyed monsters, dwarfs, a nation of Amazon women, and other peculiarly populated countries. Beliefs of this kind had been spread hundreds of years earlier by Marco Polo and Sir John Manderville, whose tales about fantastic distant lands had been known to the Spanish and Portuguese explorers and which continued to appear on some Japanese maps until the middle of the nineteenth century.

When Japan isolated itself from the world, it depended for its security upon the sea around it. But during the generations of isolation, first clipper ships, then steam ships and new knowledge of navigation and geography were drawing the world closer together and making the islands of Japan more vulnerable. Toward the middle of the nineteenth century the nation finally realized that it had put too much faith in the protection afforded by the sea, that instead of a bulwark against attack every port was vulnerable to modern ships and armaments.

TRANSITION PERIOD 1853-1868

End of isolation as U. S. "black ships" arrive to demand opening of country to trade....Shōgunate attacked for its compliance with foreign demands....Japanese enthusiastically adopt western scientific developments....Trade agreements with U. S., Russia, France, England, Holland....Movement to restore Emperor....Central government formed with young Emperor Meiji as ruler.

HISTORICAL CHRONOLOGY		ART CHRONOLOGY	
1854	Second visit of Commodore Perry with six ships; Kanagawa Treaty with the United States	1854	Sketches of Perry's squadron
		1855	Print of Kantō earthquake at Edo
1856	Consul General Townsend Harris arrives at Shimoda; office for the study of barbarian books established	1857	Kawakami Tōgai appointed inspector of painting to study western painting methods
1858	Commercial Treaty concluded; Keio University founded by Fukuzawa Yūkichi	1857-8	Painting of Townsend Harris' audience with the Shōgun
1859	Yokohama, Nagasaki and Hakodate ports open to foreign trade	1858	Hiroshige dies, memorial portrait print as Buddhist lay monk by Kunisada
1860	Japanese embassy to the United States	c. 1860	Reizei Tamechika's scrolls of Genji monogatari and Makura-no Sōshi in attempt to restore the style of the Heian period as the "national style."
1862	Japanese embassy to Europe		
1863-4	Chōshū fires on foreign ships; foreigners retaliate	1861	Japanese builders appointed contractors to foreign settlement in Yokohama; wood block print by Hōtō of Japanese sumō wrestler defeating a foreigner; Teishū's wood block print of foreign trade house in Yokohama
1865	Imperial ratification of foreign treaties		
1866	Shōgunate of Tokugawa Yoshinobu		
1867	End of Shōgunate and return of its power to the throne; Meiji Emperor enthroned	1864	Oura church built in Nagasaki
		1867	Stone cotton mill built in Kagoshima

TIME OF TRANSITION

Along the shore, temple bells and signal fires that had been lighted so many times before warned of the approach of four large, black ships flying a foreign flag.

They were United States warships commanded by Commodore Matthew C. Perry. The Japanese had been expecting him, having been notified of his earlier arrival in Okinawa. Ashore, Perry had little difficulty delivering a letter of greeting from President Millard Fillmore to representatives of the Shōgunate for delivery to the Shōgun.

Perry delivered a second letter at the same time. It contained no overt threat, but pointed out the necessity for a change in the isolationist policy of the Japanese government, especially regarding the treatment of shipwrecked American seamen (who had usually been imprisoned or executed), the opening of some ports for watering and fueling, and the placing of an American diplomatic representative in Japan. His letter further explained that he would return in the spring of the next year, when he hoped to receive an affirmative answer. Japanese authorities were certain that he was prepared to use force on his return and were sadly conscious of their completely defenseless position.

An early Japanese sketch shows the six black ships of Commodore Perry's expedition anchored off the harbor of Uraga.

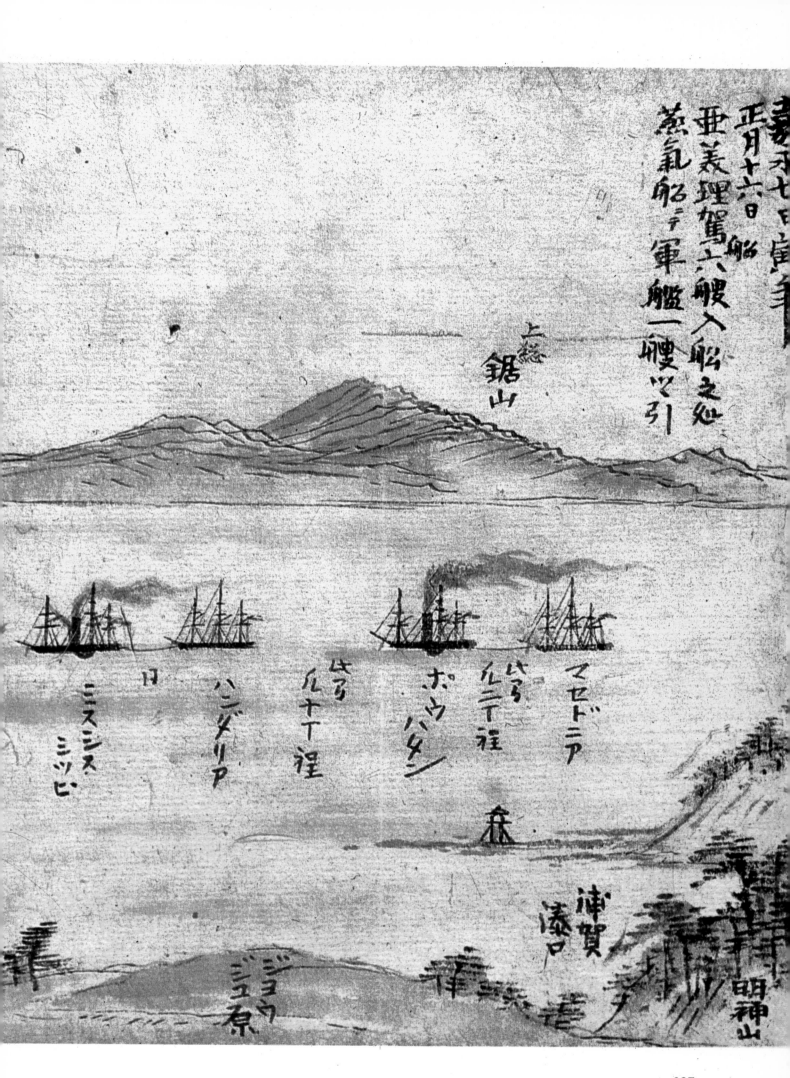

嘉永七甲寅年
正月十六日船
亜美理駕六艘入船之処
蒸氣船ニテ軍艦一艘ヲ引

上総
鋸山

ニスシス
ミッヒ

日

ハンゾメリア

此弓
九十丁程

ホウ
ハタシ

此弓
九二丁程

マセドニア

森

津賀
湊口

ジョウ
ジュ原

明神山

Red stripe around the ship at left identifies it as Commodore Perry's flagship Powhattan. Ships carried heavy armaments.

THE FIRST TREATY

When Commodore Perry and his squadron, now numbering six powerful vessels, returned to Japan, the Commodore and his officers consummated their mission with delicacy and skill. During the next few weeks a treaty was effectively concluded opening the small ports of Shimoda and Hakodate for limited trading and allowing permanent United States diplomatic representation. Other nations quickly received the benefits of United States diplomacy. Within a year, similar treaties were signed with Great Britain, Russia and Holland.

During negotiations with the Shōgunate, the Americans utilized diplomacy by revelry. They wined and dined the Japanese diplomats aboard ship, and entertained them with a hilarious minstrel show. The black faces, ragtime music, strange costumes and dances seemed incredible to the Japanese diplomats but no more so than the violent *sumō* wrestling matches featuring seminude 300-pound athletes seemed to the Americans. Diplomacy by revelry was effective. The Japanese understood and reacted immedi-

ately and favorably. Toasts of friendship were offered in *sake,* champagne and whisky.

With the signing of the treaty, Commodore Perry felt a great sense of accomplishment. Before embarking upon the expedition, he had put his views in writing showing how high he valued the importance of his mission.

"When we look at the possessions on the east of our great maritime rival, England, and of the constant and rapid increase of their fortified ports, we should be admonished of the necessity of prompt measures on our part ... Fortunately, the Japanese and many other islands of the Pacific are still left untouched ... and some of them lay in the route of a great commerce which is destined to become of great importance to the United States. No time should be lost in adopting active measures to secure a sufficient number of ports of refuge."

To implement the Perry treaty, which was little more than an amity agreement, the United States dispatched an astute diplomat, Townsend Harris, who was empowered to negotiate the first commercial treaty. By the time Harris arrived, an adverse reaction to foreigners had set

通弁官 ウリヤムス 日本出

副使 協台亜唄 アータンス

亜墨利加合衆国 使節彼理 四十六歳 こうらうせ

in. But four years after Perry's negotiations, he managed to get the treaty signed. Commercial treaties were also finalized with other countries; all were highly favorable to the foreigners. Over the next few years, they had unfortunate effects on the Japanese economy. The country became flooded with foreign goods. The outflow of gold to pay for increasing imports depleted the Shōgunate treasury. In addition, the treasury was being drained by the necessary construction of western style defenses as well as indemnities for Japanese attacks on foreigners—which were becoming frequent.

A combination of these factors, together with an inability to bring together the progressive internationalists, traditional isolationists and the restorationists, led to the ultimate downfall of the Tokugawa Shōgunate.

▼ *Minstrel show supplied as entertainment for Japanese diplomats included singers, dancers, comedians, and musicians.*

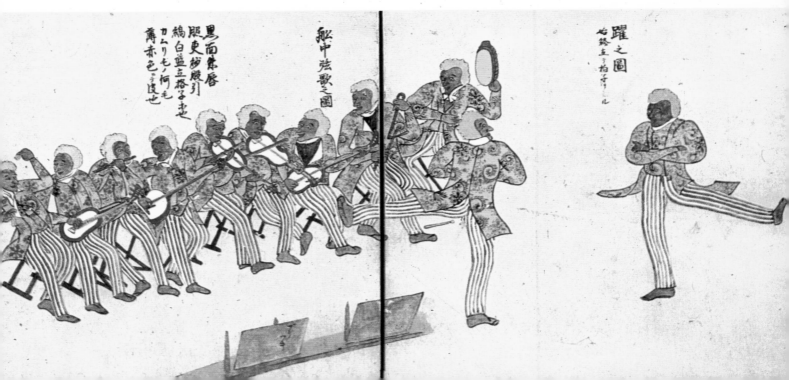

Of great interest to Japanese artists and diplomatic representatives were uniforms and swords worn by U.S. officers.

STRANGERS BEARING GIFTS

The Americans lavished a great array of gifts on the Japanese, items chosen with care. They brought rifles, pistols and swords, a wide selection of potent alcoholic drinks—cordials, wines, and a hundred gallons of American whiskey.

The pistols and rifles were especially well received by the intensely interested and quietly enthusiastic diplomats. The Americans also presented the sending and receiving sections of the newly invented telegraph instrument, a collection of John Audubon's famous bird prints and a copy of Webster's dictionary. The Japanese were greatly intrigued by a camera, the first ever

▼ *Tools, guns, and the telegraph, were brought to Japan as gifts. Not shown are the pistols which became prized possessions.*

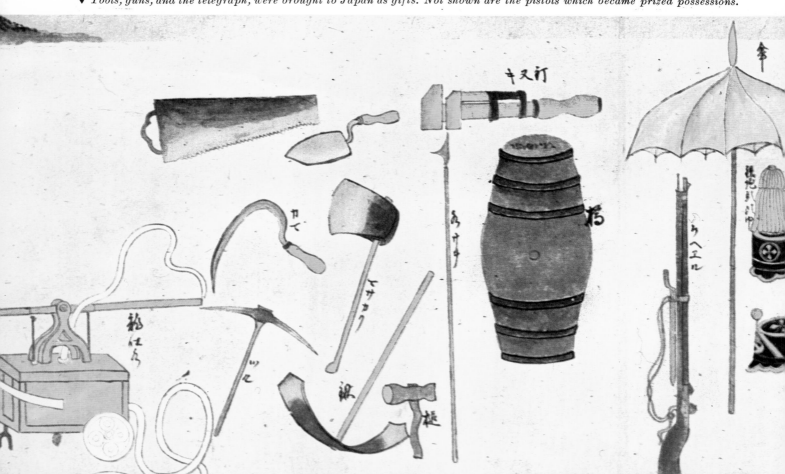

Most impressive present was the working steam engine shown in detailed sketch by Japanese artist. Note date, 1853.

seen in that country. They also showed great interest in the military dress uniforms worn by the American officers.

The largest and most impressive item in the gift exchange, the one that excited the Japanese most, was a completely operating steam locomotive built in miniature. With it came the necessary rails, tender and passenger cars. After set-

ting up this mechanical marvel, the Americans took the diplomats on their first train ride.

For their part, the Japanese reciprocated with gifts to the Americans, all in keeping with their tradition of peaceful isolation. Among them were expensive and intricately woven silk brocades, gold and silver inlaid lacquer boxes and cases, and delicate objects of porcelain.

▼ *Japanese were interested in camera and strange band instruments. Whiskey, wine and cordials were happily accepted.*

THE GREAT
EDO
EARTHQUAKE

A devastating earthquake struck Japan in 1855. Thousands were killed; many cities and villages were destroyed. The population of the country—then approximately 30 million—was just recovering from the effects of a previous earthquake a few months earlier.

Edo, the capital, was especially hard hit by the second catastrophe. Uncontrollable fires raged through the city consuming the flimsy wooden structures and even destroying large earthen-walled warehouses where food was stored.

The effects of this holocaust were reported daily over a period of weeks in the newspapers of the time called *kawara-ban*. Usually distributed by book shops, large sheets were printed by wood block. More than 400 editions dealing

On November 11, 1855, a great earthquake destroyed much of the Kantō district. The crowded city of Edo suffered most.

with the earthquake and its aftereffects were printed. These papers, which gave the Japanese their first regular news, also reported such events as suicides, plots dealing with revenge as well as natural disasters and battles. Rumors were also a favorite subject, and fantastic stories helped circulation. A great many copies were sold during the earthquake when the paper at-tributed the disaster to a sea monster.

The second largest edition ever printed was devoted to a series of devastating floods along the famed Tōkaidō Road. Toward the end of the Tokugawa period, readers began a clamor for news of the foreigners in Japan, a demand satis-fied to a degree by this early form of pictorial journalism.

235

THE PUBLIC BATHS

Cleanliness has always been a part of religious ritual among the Japanese people. Every object used in Shintō ceremonies must be scrupulously clean. Outside each Shintō shrine is a trough of clean water, where the worshiper may wash his hands and mouth. It is probable that the passion for cleanliness among the Japanese had its origins in their religion.

By the middle of the eighteenth century public bathing had become a social occasion as well as an opportunity to soak out tired muscles in hot water and cleanse the body by scouring with a rough sponge. Literally thousands of public baths were available, many of them catering to

236

Inside public bathhouse women of all ages are seen. The bathhouse manager at right is attempting to quiet disturbance.

women exclusively, others only to men. In the great majority washing rooms for men and women were separate, but after washing, soaking in the big, hot pool was enjoyed by both sexes. Some of the large baths in the city could hold a hundred or more.

In the country areas natural hot springs were popular with bathers. Many people traveled to these spas believing that the waters of different springs possessed different curative powers. Some were believed to be good for bad eyesight, others for rheumatism and still others for skin infections. Around these spas resorts blossomed. Many became famous throughout the nation.

THE PATIENT
CONSUL GENERAL

The first United States Consul General to Japan, Townsend Harris, was a patient but determined diplomat. His arrival in 1856 caused the Japanese almost as much consternation as Perry's three years earlier.

He was first informed that there was no purpose in his being there; that the United States did not need representation. He was urged to go home. By this time, criticism of the Shōgunate for their acquiescence to the treaty negotiated by Commodore Perry had set in. The idea of a permanent diplomatic United States representative, which would inevitably be followed by representatives from other countries, was resisted vigorously.

So for the next few months Townsend Harris got nowhere in his efforts to meet with and deliver his credentials to the Shōgun. Evasions were ingenious and continuous. When he wrote to the Shōgunate, he was told that it was not the custom of the government to reply to the letters of foreigners. No one from the least to the most important official wanted to be involved.

The Tokugawa Shōgunate was fighting for its very existence against the restorationists and any advantage given to a foreigner weakened their position. Harris was, therefore, given every opportunity to give up his seemingly futile mission. His interpreter was assassinated and he himself often threatened. But he continued to importune the government for an audience. On December 7, 1857 after the British had fired on Canton in China and after the Japanese had learned that United States forces, after being attacked by the Chinese, had retaliated by firing on the forts surrounding Canton, the Shōgunate realized that a continuation of their evasive tactics and further delay might bring negotiation by force to Japan. The Shōgunate arranged a meeting with Townsend Harris.

Harris successfully carried out the negotiations and on July 29, 1858 the final treaty was signed. It provided for diplomatic and consular privileges including extra-territorial l e g a l rights (allowing foreign citizens to be judged by their own laws) and a fixed tariff at low rates as well as the opening of a number of ports. Similar treaties were signed within the next few months with England, France, Holland and Russia.

After a long wait, Consul Townsend Harris had audience with Shōgun Iesada. This meeting led to first commercial treaty.

THE TRADING PORTS

When the ports of Yokohama, Nagasaki and Hakodate were officially opened to foreign trade, their growth from fishing villages to thriving communities was rapid. Of the three, Yokohama, blessed with an excellent deep harbor and located close to the capital at Edo, showed the greatest gain in population. Custom houses, warehouses, waterfront dockyards and residences in the new foreign settlement rose almost overnight. Soon the waterfront took on some of the

aspects of such foreign ports as Hong Kong and Shanghai as British and Scottish traders constructed houses in much the same way as other Englishmen had in China.

Behind high gates foreign diplomats and traders lived, as nearly as possible, the way they had at home. Only in the crowded streets outside the gates or at official functions did the foreigners come in contact with the Japanese.

Procuring food for the foreigners created a

Because of its fine, deep harbor and proximity to Edo, Yokohama became Japan's most important foreign port.
▼ *Activity at the wharf in Yokohama harbor shows commercial traffic moving in and out of the busy customs area.*

considerable problem. Much of it had to be imported, for to the Japanese people meat eating was a vulgar and abhorrent idea which they took to very slowly. However, around 1860 the Japanese must have tried frying beef with bean curd, soya extract and local vegetables, for such a concoction caught on and was soon known in trading ports as *sukiyaki*. Before many years had passed, it had developed an international reputation as a typical Japanese dish.

THE BLACK SHIPS

After the signing of the trade treaty, many "black ships" as most foreign trading vessels were called, were anchored in the treaty harbors. Merchants from most European countries as well as the United States were anxious to get in at the beginning of trade with Japan. The ports of Yokohama and Nagasaki were crowded with ships of all countries and sizes carrying traders, missionaries (although they were not yet legally qualified to enter the country) and adventurers of all kinds. It was the culmination of the many years spent by the West trying to open the doors to trade with the Japanese.

The endeavor started with the English whose attempts to open trade relations after Japan had sealed itself off were unsuccessful. They were followed by Russian envoys: Laksman in 1792 and Rezanov in 1804. Then the British came again during the war between England and Holland. The United States made two attempts. First came the unarmed *Morrison* with a shipload of missionaries and Japanese castaways being brought back for repatriation. They were fired upon and driven off, but this incident probably helped in having the edict of *uchihcrai* (drive the foreigner away) revoked. The matter was taken quite seriously by the governments of the United States, England and Russia, as well as the government of Japan. The United States and Russia were especially concerned for both had extensive whaling interests in the North Pacific. On numerous occasions whaling ships and crews in distress had been turned away from shore or attacked when driven close to the Japanese Islands.

Busy scene in Yokohama harbor shows early travelers who came to Japan in the "black ships" in the transition era.

Long after the edict was modified, two United States warships under the command of Commodore James Biddle arrived and were well treated. Biddle requested that trade treaty negotiations be opened. The Shōgunate refused and the Americans withdrew.

When the trade treaty was finally ratified, foreign ships sailed in ever-increasing numbers and the foreign colony grew rapidly. The Japanese were both repelled by and interested in the foreign ships. They resented the foreigners being on their soil but had a great curiosity about the ships' fittings, their guns, their steam power and the odd customs of the western people.

帆柱ニ上リ
又ハ海中ニ
入役ナリ

但シ
是ハ黒人國ヨリ雇來ルヨシ

船号シススケンサ
ト云

船長サ四十五間
幅十六間
車八間
衆人但シ水三艘
三百人

REACTION TO THE FOREIGNERS

The cry of *son-nō* (revere the Emperor) began to
be heard throughout the country. As the reaction
by the Japanese to the first traders became violent, it became *son-nō-jōi* (revere the Emperor,
expel the barbarians).

Reasons for anti-foreign reaction were easy to
find. The foreigners had no understanding of
Japanese traditions and violated many of them.
Another of the objections was that they bought
up Japanese gold, causing a rise in local prices.

But the uprisings were not all the fault of the
foreigners. Thousands of out-of-work samurai,
trained to defend the isolationist traditions of
their country, found not only the presence but
also the customs of the foreigners repulsive.
Some demonstrated their feelings by physical
attacks. Others were content to ignore the foreigners or refused to cooperate with them. Fortunately, most of their energies were channeled
into the cause of restoring power to the Emper-
or, in the hope that he would re-establish their
status and expel the foreigners.

Not all the reaction was unfavorable. Most
Japanese were gracious, hospitable, helpful,
and quite naturally curious about the odd dress
and strange manner of the newcomers.

244

Wood-block print of a Russian vessel shows the ship as a sea monster. Caricatures of individuals are of the Russian crew.

▼ *Fashionable European ladies receive curious looks from Japanese ladies and gentlemen as they enter the settlement.*

PARTIES AND PARADES

When the foreign settlements were opened, merchants, sailors, and soldiers attached to the British, French, Russian, Dutch and American legations formed the nucleus for a distinctive Western-Japanese culture. In early settlement days, foreign vessels came not only to trade but to refuel, take on water and replenish their food stocks. In addition to the traders, many adventurers came to the settlements in the hope of making a quick fortune. One enterprising gentleman imported overland coaches fully expecting to use them as transport to the gold mines. Because gold mining was rigidly controlled and there was no opportunity for foreigners to stake out claims, the stage coaches were ultimately used on a pioneer run from Yokohama to Edo.

Soldiers from the foreign countries, with few exceptions, were well received by the Japanese military and the residents of the "concession" ports. Foreign military bands were especially popular, judging from the great number of *nishiki-e*, wood-block prints printed and distributed in great numbers. These prints, developed from the earlier *ukiyo-e* prints, were first created by Suzuki Harunobu in the mid-eighteenth century. By the time of the opening of the settlement ports, *nishiki-e* had declined considerably in artistic quality, yet the *nishiki-e* artist pro-

◄ *Parades by foreigners were frequent events along the waterfront of Yokohama and were often sketched by Japanese artists.*

▼ *Foreigners representing five different countries watch as a Chinese magician entertains in a Yokohama geisha house.*

Gay dance is done by a foreigner in Yokohama restaurant. On table, in foreground, is sake flask and a fish called tai.
▶ *Japanese sumō wrestler is shown defeating a foreigner. This print symbolizes the early reaction against foreigners.*

duced a vivid record of the contemporary scene.

Based upon these colorful pictures, it is apparent that foreigners in Japan enjoyed the food, entertainment and company of the Japanese. Fish, ducks and various types of wild birds were plentiful and cheap. *Sake* was readily available, and there were plenty of geisha ready to pour it. These entertainers specialized in dancing, singing, the playing of the *samisen* and companionship at the dinner table. They should not be confused with the *oiran* (prostitutes), who were attractive and available.

北亞墨利加
合衆國

假石垣
蕾文記

一川芳員画

共和政治合衆國と称せる者三十一州北亞墨利加の名は此極未生多ぶらぶらさる地より南部を宇華堂に至る迄の總称そう合衆國っアメリカの一部とく出するそれ地共大にして人民過多それ勢も亦最も旺盛さると以て今単れでの地を通称して北アメリカ之芸迄年國勢倍々加もり其近國此盟社か來會せしゞ土産他邦に倍に者挙て算べうゞ國民義気なりて天地の理学武備商交を専らとせち婦人優みて又美なり

It was in the field of entertainment that Japanese and foreigners met most easily. Traditionally taught to cope with any entertainment situation, the geisha soon charmed the visitors. In this area, there was no language nor custom barrier. Americans, British, French and Russians danced, sang and drank with their gracious and acquiescent hostesses. Because the foreigners could not visit the famous Yoshiwara gay quarter, it came to the settlements.

Within and around the settlements, many Japanese adopted western dress, although not completely, for western clothing was expensive. It was not unusual to see Japanese dressed in western shoes, derby hats, but in the traditional *hakama*. Artisans observed the work of western carpenters, plumbers and sail makers and were quick to adopt useful techniques.

▲ *American mother feeds baby while father proudly shows watch. Western watches, new to Japan, were very popular.*
◄ *American displays his watch as his wife uses an early model of sewing machine. Text describes the United States.*
► *Dapper Dutchman using a telescope was imaginatively sketched by Japanese artist who elongated subject and chair.*

おろしや人の圖

海上
一万四千三百里

Russian soldiers, sailors and merchants were frequent visitors to Japan. Above, Russian rides spirited horse.

252

Horseback was important method of transport in the 1860's. Chinese rides near Kanagawa, district adjoining Tokyo.

END OF THE FEUDAL STATE

The end of the Tokugawa Shōgunate and the restoration of power to the throne was forecast in events that occurred on the Tōkaidō Road between 1863 and 1868. The winding road, stretching between Edo and Kyoto, became unusually heavy with traffic when the Tokugawa Shōgunate relaxed its authority, no longer insisting on the regular attendance of the vassal lords in the capital. At the same time, hostage families were allowed to return to their own domains. For the next few months, a great procession of lords, ladies and retainers traveled the road to their home estates. Following them came a high percentage of the population of the capital.

Shortly after this, along the same road, came the fourteenth Tokugawa Shōgun himself, accompanied by some 3,000 retainers, a procession that was an even surer sign of the diminishing influence of the Shōgunate. For the Shōgun was

Soldiers of the Tokugawa Shōgunate in feudal regalia shoot a cannon across three panels of this unique wood-block print.

on his way to consult with the Emperor at the Imperial Court in Kyoto, the first time a Tokugawa Shōgun was to humble himself before the Imperial Court. Two and a half centuries earlier, a Shōgun had traveled East in triumph— with a retinue ten times as large.

At the Imperial Court, the Shōgun succumbed to pressure by powerful lords close to the throne. When he traveled back to Edo, he was shorn of much of his power.

The final downfall of the Shōgunate came when the important Chōshū clan revolted against Tokugawa authority. The Shōgunate moved against the rebels but the powerful Chōshū clan, led by young samurai, was victorious in almost every engagement. During this period of minor battles the Shōgun died. His successor, confronted with certain defeat and the rising movement for a central government and restoration of power to the Crown, agreed to resign.

He hoped, by stepping down in a graceful manner, that a peaceful way might be opened for

255

Foreigners watch as soldiers of the Shōgunate leave Edo to attack, unsuccessfully, the samurai of the daimyo of Chōshū.

the formation of a new government in which the Tokugawa could participate. But the dissident clans insisted upon complete supremacy over the Tokugawa and got it. After a brief civil war, the Shōgunate and vassals were compelled to submit to the rule of the newly inaugurated young Emperor whose regime later came to be known as Meiji. Soon he, with a splendid retinue, traveled triumphantly up the Tōkaidō Road from the old capital at Kyoto to the new capital at Tokyo.

MEIJI
PERIOD
1868-1912

 The charter oath....Young samurai successfully lead new government....Bicycles, first trains, telegraph....First people's army....Adoption of Constitution....Beginning of great industrial cartels, *zaibatsu*....Successful completion of war with China followed by victory over Russia....Expansion in literature, criticism and poetry....Japan emerges as world power.

HISTORICAL CHRONOLOGY		ART CHRONOLOGY	
1868	Meiji restoration; Charter Oath; Imperial capital moved to Tokyo	1872	First display of Japanese paintings abroad at the Paris World Exposition
1869	Daimyo returned domains to throne	1873	Reconstruction of the Ginza along modern lines, popularized brick construction
1870	Commoners permitted to take surnames	1876	Josiah Conder arrived as professor of architecture in Technological College
1872	First national bank; first railway; adoption of western calendar (the third of the twelfth month of the fifth year of Meiji as January 1, 1873)	1878	Ernest Fenollosa came as professor to Tokyo University
1873	Land tax reform; universal military service	1879	Formation of Ryūchi Society which advocated a return to the appreciation of traditional art
1877	Satsuma Rebellion; Tokyo University founded	1882	Ueno Museum in Tokyo opened
1879	Ex-President Ulysses Simpson Grant visited Japan	1883	The Rokumeikan Hall built
1889	Promulgation of the Constitution	1887	Government art school opened
1890	First Diet opened; Imperial rescripts on education	1895	Sino-Japanese War painting by Kiyochika; Kyoto Museum constructed, Katayama Tōkuma the architect
1894-5	Sino-Japanese War	1897	Painting, "By the Lakeside," by Kuroda Seiki after his return from France in 1893
1897	Adoption of gold standard	1903	Fifth National Industrial Fair
1902	Ango-Japanese alliance signed	1909	Akasaka Detached Palace completed
1904-5	Russo-Japanese War	1912	Print of funeral procession of Meiji Emperor by Hampo
1910	Annexation of Korea		
1912	Death of Meiji Emperor, succession of his son Yoshihito		

Acting independently, Yamaoka Tesshū, vassal of the Shōgun, rode from Edo to Shizuoka to meet the army of the Emperor

THE NEW JAPAN

With the inauguration of the "enlightened rule" period which the Emperor's progressive regime was then named, Japan emerged from the world of the past into the world of the present. The young Emperor was a fifteen-year-old boy, but he was fortunate in having as advisors a group of men willing and able to shape the course of the new Japan. Working enthusiastically, they brought about a relatively smooth amalgamation of eastern and western cultures.

Most of these ministers (many were quite young) came from the samurai class. All had been reared in the warrior tradition of responsibility and leadership. Some, who now pushed for the adoption of western methods, had fought for the expulsion of the foreigners in their effort to destroy the Tokugawa Shōgunate and restore the Emperor. Now, realizing that Japan must

led by Saigo. He successfully proposed that the attack on Edo be postponed until a peace conference could be arranged.

play an international role in the world, they were united in looking towards the West. They hoped to adapt western ideas while retaining the values of the East. As one of their spiritual predecessors, Sakuma Shōzan, wrote: "eastern ethics and western science."

Throughout the new government all efforts were directed toward improving the economy of the country and toward building up its military strength. Yet the emphasis on arming, so that the country could negotiate on equal terms with the rest of the world, was not done at the expense of the welfare of the whole country. The government respected the interests of merchants, former feudal estate owners, farmers and samurai. Foreign experts in transportation, defense, agriculture and industry were employed and their progressive methods carefully studied and adopted. A program of social reform was put into motion. Education was made compulsory and, by the end of the Meiji period, attendance in schools stood at ninety-eight per cent.

259

As the young Emperor grew older, he continued to rely on his ministers for advice. Yet in an unobtrusive manner he exerted a moderating influence. Reared in Kyoto in seclusion, he was content to remain in the background but through his dignity and wise counsel, he gave the throne a stature it had not known for hundreds of years.

While the country embarked upon new ways, the Imperial Court emphasized traditional ethical values based on Confucian philosophy deeply ingrained in the Japanese character.

Inevitably, there were monumental difficulties to overcome in the changeover from feudalism to a central government. And there were minor rebellions and deep disagreements among the ministers. But none of these was allowed to disrupt the march of progress. The government of Japan slowly at first, then with increasing speed, earned the respect of the world.

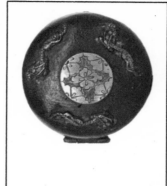
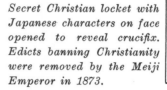

Secret Christian locket with Japanese characters on face opened to reveal crucifix. Edicts banning Christianity were removed by the Meiji Emperor in 1873.

▲ *Japan's first commercial bank was this structure owned by the Mitsui family. It was located in business center of Edo.*
◄ *In early Meiji telegraph wires were strung on living trees from Tokyo to Kyoto. Beneath wires is a roadside teahouse.*

Famous Tokyo bridge was the terminus of all highways leading into the city. Regulations and edicts were posted on wooden

billboard structure at left. Bicycles had recently been introduced into Japan. There were said to be 50,000 jinrikisha.

TRAINS RUN ON TIME

The miniature steam engine that had been presented to the Japanese government at the time of Admiral Perry's arrival in 1853 had made a deep impression. Even before the fall of the Tokugawa Shōgunate steam engines had been ordered. The first train route was to be between Kyoto and Tokyo. But a series of unforeseen difficulties delayed the track laying between the old and new capitals, and Yokohama, which had become the most important trading center, became the terminus of the first railroad.

Only four years after ascending the throne in 1868, the nineteen-year-old Meiji Emperor was able to make the first trip by train from Shimbashi Station in Tokyo to Yokohama. The trip at that time took 53 minutes. The inaugural run, however, was made in considerably less time. The British engineer was determined to show

First railroad ran from Tokyo to Yokohama. Lettering at top is train schedules and ticket prices. Trip took 53 minutes.

how much speed he could get from his engine. The train carrying the Emperor and his entourage arrived in Yokohama before arrangements had been completed to receive them. Instead of congratulations upon his record-breaking trip, the engineer received a severe reprimand.

Accounts of early train rides inevitably include anecdotes about passengers. Many, observing the traditional ritual of removing one's shoes when entering a house, left their shoes on the platform when they entered the train and regretfully watched them disappear as the train departed.

Other transportation kept pace. Horse-drawn carriages and street cars, bicycles, and the recently invented *jinrikisha*, competed with hand-carried palanquins and ancient oxcarts. Traffic was especially heavy in Tokyo on the street called Ginza which became the first cobblestone thoroughfare.

265

INDUSTRIAL BEGINNINGS

The young Meiji government worked hard to balance production for domestic use as well as for export. Protection for native industries was a prime consideration, but the new internationalists understood the necessity for an accelerated industrial revolution in Japan. They were quick to adopt western methods in heavy industries and in the processing of textiles.

The foundations for some of the great fortunes of Japan were laid in the early Meiji period, when the government, after nationalizing and developing such industries as shipbuilding, mining, railroads, electricity and silk and cotton mills, sold them to merchant contractors *(sei-shō)*, who operated them as independent enter-

prises. This was the beginning of the Mitsubishi, Mitsui and Sumitomo fortunes and the birth of the great Zaibatsu organizations. The development of these corporations into powerful industrial combines was based upon tight family control, the general economic growth of the country and the demand for consumer goods when a wave of prosperity came to Japan after the war with China.

The war, while not entirely successful, opened new markets for Japan in Formosa and Mongolia. A few years later, the war with Russia, which was a success, brought additional markets. As these areas were opened to Japanese goods, domestic markets increased. By 1905, Japan was able to compete successfully with western goods in many Asian markets.

267

SATSUMA REBELLION

The first test of the young Meiji government came with the revolt of the powerful Satsuma clan based in the southern region of the island of Kyūshū. This influential clan was headed by the Shimazu family, which had been founded by Shimazu Tadahisa, son of Minamoto Yoritomo, in the Kamakura period. It was one of the two powerful clans (the other was the Chōshū) that

◄ *Famous correspondent Fukuchi Genichirō reports Satsuma Rebellion. Recently-formed government army fords river.*

made the restoration of power to the Emperor possible.

After nine years of working close to the central government, the samurai of Satsuma had grown dissatisfied with the direction the government was taking. They organized a considerable army to fight against the untried troops of the central government. It was a momentous clash between traditional Japanese warfare, as waged by the sword-wielding individual warriors, and the new peasant army, trained in western strategy and using western weapons.

The rebellion was led by Saigō Takamori, a giant of a man with an engaging personality who, just a few years earlier, had been a leader in the government and who, as field marshall, had

Brave women from the island of Kyūshū formed an army in order to fight against government troops in the Satsuma Rebellion. Their weapons are traditional naginata *(long-handled sword) and were used against the government cavalry attack.*

actually been responsible for forming the government army that he now opposed. Saigō was one of the three young samurai who had joined the government and whose personal magnetism had helped to weld it together. The second was Kido Kōin, a samurai from the Chōshū clan, who was an extraordinarily able diplomat, a master of the art of persuasion. Kido's historical importance rests primarily upon his conviction that feudalism had to be abolished if the nation was to prosper together with his ability to con-

vince the feudal lords that it was in their own interests, as well as their patriotic duty, to return the Emperor to power and to support the new central government. The third of the triumvirate was Ōkubo Toshimichi who, as Saigō, was also a member of the Satsuma clan. Saigō was the impetuous man of action, Kido the diplomat, and Ōkubo the master planner of the new regime. Later it was because of the opposition of Ōkubo to Saigō's ideas for conquest and expansion that Saigō resigned from the government. Saigō had

Mixup in telegram led to erroneous print of Saigō committing seppuku *at sea. Actual suicide occurred on a mountaintop.*

advanced a plan for the conquest of Korea that included sending an envoy to that country to make impossible and insulting demands. This would result, he explained, in the Koreans executing the envoy and would thereby give Japan an excuse for declaring war. The envoy, he insisted, would be himself. Ōkubo and Kido refused him, and Saigō went back to his home in Kyūshū. There, he was prevailed upon to join the rebellious samurai and to lead them against the government army.

The government acted swiftly to crush the rebellion. The fighting was brief but bloody. Saigō and his men fought well, but the government soldiers easily triumphed. When he was badly wounded, he committed suicide in the samurai tradition, rather than be captured. But his contribution to the early government, his bravery and spirit were not forgotten. He became a hero to future Japanese soldiers and was pardoned posthumously by the Meiji Emperor, whom he had both supported and opposed.

271

FIRST INDUSTRIAL FAIR

The new Japanese navy band, resplendent in western uniforms, played at the inaugural ceremony of Japan's first industrial fair. The Em-

peror and Empress arrived in their royal coaches to open the exposition. The year was 1877, the tenth year of the reign of the Meiji Emperor. The fair was located at Ueno, notable as the site of the Kan-enji Buddhist temple.

It illustrated the remarkable progress made in

Daring nishiki-e wood-block print shows faces of Meiji Emperor and Empress as they attend first trade fair.

the nine years since the reformation of the central government. The Japanese government had participated in the international fairs of Vienna in 1873 and of Philadelphia in 1876 and had felt the need of a trade show of their own.

The emphasis was on industry, for the promoters of the fair hoped to show that Japan's craftsmen and industrial designers could produce western-type goods as well as traditional Japanese items. The fair lasted for 102 days and was a great success. Six more such industrial expositions were held during the Meiji period.

273

The Ex-President of the United States Ulysses Simpson Grant visited Japan in 1879. He was entertained royally at

an elaborate affair given in his honor. Seated at the left of the General and his wife are the Emperor and Empress of Japan.

DANCING AND DIPLOMACY

Up until the late Meiji period, party dresses were not a social problem for the Japanese woman. She wore her seasonal kimono and, by tradition, rarely attended parties, certainly never parties where foreign gentlemen and their ladies were likely to be present. But foreign minister Inoue Kaoru attempted to change this with a policy of entertaining foreigners in western style. His elaborate plan called for the construction of a special building which was called *Rokumeikan.*

Inoue's idea of entertaining foreign guests in their own fashion was not strictly for social reasons. He, along with other Japanese ministers, believed that foreign dignitaries and members of legations would be more likely to accept revisions to inequable trade agreements made by Japan when the country was opened. These treaties, signed at a time when Japan was in no position to bargain, were decidedly favorable to the foreign countries and a source of continuous irritation. And so it was that a small number of Japanese women got their first western party dresses. With the importation of the sewing machine, the number of western dresses available increased rapidly and a whole new dressmaking (*yōsai*) industry was formed.

The elaborate parties had no effect upon treaty revision. This fact, added to the expense and disregard of established convention, brought this style of diplomacy into disrepute and ultimately caused the resignation of foreign minister Inoue. The new foreign minister, Okuma, believed that dancing and fancy dress balls were the province of businessmen, not of the Japanese government.

◄ *Japanese ladies took naturally to western fashions which became very popular in Tokyo in the eighties and nineties.*
▼ *Making of western-style dresses became an early home industry in the Meiji period. Sewing machines were a vital import.*

THE FIRST CONSTITUTION

Japan's first constitution was not an imitation of any foreign charter. Unlike western constitutions, its base rested on the principle of a divine emperor, an absolute ruler and deity whose sovereignty was unquestioned. But it did provide for a parliament, the Diet, consisting of two houses, the nobles and, in theory, the commoners.

The father of the Japanese constitution was Ito Hirobumi, who had been appointed by the Emperor in 1881 to draft it. His knowledge of western government began when he defied the edict of the Tokugawa government and sailed to Europe while the country was technically closed. Later trips were made as a government envoy.

Ito worked on his draft of the constitution for a total of eight years. Feeling that it should be shaped to the traditions of the country, he was in no hurry to adopt an unworkable system. When finally presented in 1889, it represented an unlimited monarchy, for all ministers of state as well as heads of the army and navy reported directly to the Emperor rather than to the Diet representatives.

Yet, limited thought it was, Ito's constitution was the beginning of representative government in Japan based upon law, and it added measurably to Japan's growing prestige in the world.

▶ *A great event in Japanese history occurred in 1889 when the Emperor Meiji presented the first Imperial constitution.*
▼ *First session of the parliament meets with the Emperor, top center. Many famous Japanese statesmen can be identified.*

WAR
WITH CHINA

After successful campaign in Manchuria, Japanese invade North China peninsula. Army landed from boats imbedded in ice.
▼ To observe enemy movements, Sino-Japanese War hero swam a wide river in central Korea carrying a sword in his mouth.

威海衛攻撃
氷上之進軍

The war between China and Japan had its beginnings in Korea. China claimed suzerainty over the peninsula, but Japan enjoyed favorable trade relations with Korea and resented China's growing influence. A revolt in Korea, followed by the movement of Chinese troops going to the aid of the Korean king, provided Japan with a sought-after opportunity to intervene and to demand that China evacuate the peninsula.

In July 1894, the Japanese began the war by sinking a Chinese troopship, and during the next nine months proceeded to force the Chinese army out of Korea. The victorious and well-organized Japanese then proceeded to take the Liaotung Peninsula and to capture the North China harbor of Port Arthur during the following eight months.

The war was over in less than a year. In April 1895, China ceded Formosa, the Pescadores Islands, Port Arthur and the Liaotung Peninsula at the southern tip of Manchuria and recognized the complete independence of Korea.

But Japan was not to be allowed the fruits of victory. The powerful western countries of France, Russia and Germany exerted immediate pressure, forcing her to give up the Liaotung Peninsula as well as the harbor and fortress of Port Arthur. Left without a choice, for Japan was in no position to oppose these powers, the Meiji Emperor accepted the demands on behalf of the embittered country.

There was much righteous anger during the ensuing years directed against these western nations, for each of them seized, leased or annexed Chinese territories to themselves. France moved into Kwangchow in South China; the Germans took control of Tsingtao and Kiaochow; while Russia occupied Port Arthur and the Liaotung Peninsula. This Russian move was to become one of the causes of the Russo-Japanese War.

WAR WITH RUSSIA

Again Korea served as a steppingstone to war. Russian influence was growing fast in that country, and combined with Russian control of Port Arthur and the Liaotung Peninsula, Japan's trading areas were severely threatened. An alliance with Great Britain supplied Japan with the security she needed to attack the expanding Russian outposts.

When the Russians demanded a neutral zone in Korea to begin north of the thirty-ninth parallel and insisted upon complete control of trade and resources in South Manchuria, Japan responded by discontinuing diplomatic procedures. Moving her navy into the coastal area without warning, she attacked a portion of the Russian fleet at Port Arthur. Japan declared war the next day.

The war was short, dramatic and conclusive. Because Russia was much larger and was considered a far more powerful country than Japan, world opinion considered the Japanese the "underdog", and most of the world sided with her. The Japanese army fought courageously, even brilliantly, winning one campaign after another against the dogged Russian army. In the United States, President Theodore Roosevelt did not hesitate to express his admiration for the courage of the Japanese.

The war was over in eighteen months. Fast running out of both trained soldiers and money, Japan suggested to the U.S. President that a peaceful settlement of the conflict be proposed. The treaty was signed in Portsmouth, New Hampshire. While Russia was defeated, Japan in turn was economically exhausted.

The Japanese navy destroyed a larger Russian fleet in battle of the Japan Sea. This engagement hastened end of the war.
◄ Greatest land battle of Russo-Japanese War was fought in Manchuria near city of Mukden. The armies clashed in winter.
▼ Kites were flown as the signal of the surrender of Russians at Port Arthur. The harbor had been under siege 154 days.

THE NEW FACE OF TOKYO

The face of urban Japan changed rapidly at the turn of the century. Most new construction and modernization was confined to the cities, where western and traditional architecture were combined to produce unique landmarks.

Most interesting was the *Ryōunkaku* (rising over the clouds), Tokyo's first skyscraper. The slim round edifice did indeed seem to reach to the heavens. There were twelve stories, which included three observation towers above the eighth floor and a cupola on top rising 225 feet above the ground. The first elevator to be seen in Japan was installed and operated up to the eighth floor. *Jūnikai* (twelve stories), as it was affectionately called, immediately became the most popular amusement center in Japan. It was dedicated, from basement to top, to pleasure. There were theaters, bars and restaurants on every floor.

So popular was the building that thousands of wood-block prints were made for a game called *sugoroku*, a popular pastime played by both adults and children. The player progressed upward or downward from one landing to another depending upon the throw of a die.

The area in which *Junikai* was located had long been one of Tokyo's amusement sections but with the construction of this building the district, called Asakusa, became the most important entertainment region of the city.

Other areas of Tokyo were modernized with ugly square brick shops replacing the earlier wood and *shōji* structures. Typical of this change was that on the Ginza, which became the main shopping center. Modern western-style buildings began to replace earlier structures throughout the central business district called Marunouchi, which developed almost in the shadow of the Imperial Palace. But a strong and successful effort was made to retain as much of the natural beauty as possible, and it was reflected in forested groves, parks and temple grounds.

Architectural borrowing from the West stopped in the urban areas. In towns and villages and throughout the countryside, Japanese architecture continued to develop along traditional lines.

◀ *First skyscraper was this twelve story amusement center in downtown Tokyo. It had Japan's first elevator.*
▶ *Electric lights blaze across the entrance to fifth industrial fair. Japanese and western-style clothing was worn.*

TOWARD THE FUTURE

Even before the death of the Meiji Emperor, Japan had become an important power in the modern world. Not all its gains had been made through warfare, although its victorious campaigns in China and Russia had shown other nations that Japan could defend itself and was even capable of extending its power. Clearly, the most significant advances in the late Meiji period were in industry and education. One of the earliest steps of the first representational government was to form a Ministry of Education. The first Imperial decree for the encouragement of education came in 1872, and by 1912, when the greatly respected Meiji Emperor died, most of its provisions had become fact. The decree read in part: "There shall, hereafter, be no illiterate family among the people of any community, nor shall there be an illiterate member in any family ... learning is the basis for all human endeavor from the commonplace speaking, reading, writing and calculating for everyday needs, to the professional needs of the military man, government official, farmer, merchant, craftsman and artist, in the multitude of technical skills and

Westerners and Japanese stroll in the moonlight viewing spring cherry blossoms in the Yoshiwara district of Tokyo.
▼ *Dignitaries from throughout the world attend funeral of Meiji Emperor. In his reign, Japan progressed from an isolated nation to an internationally respected world power.*

International influence is shown in a western style painting of young Japanese playing Japanese and western instruments.

arts and in law, politics and astronomy.''

One sentence in the Rescript on Education issued by the Meiji Emperor, ''Devote yourself to public service in a national emergency,'' helped to unify the Japanese people during the Sino-Japanese and Russo-Japanese Wars.

The first state educational institution, Tokyo University, was founded in 1877, and within thirty years four other universities were opened.

Japanese architecture was beginning to influence the architecture of the modern world, and Japanese painting was having a distinct influence on the evolution of the French impressionist school. Japanese industry occupied a solid and respectable position in the world market. The country, which had been an isolated and feudal state just sixty years before, had become one of the great powers of the modern world.

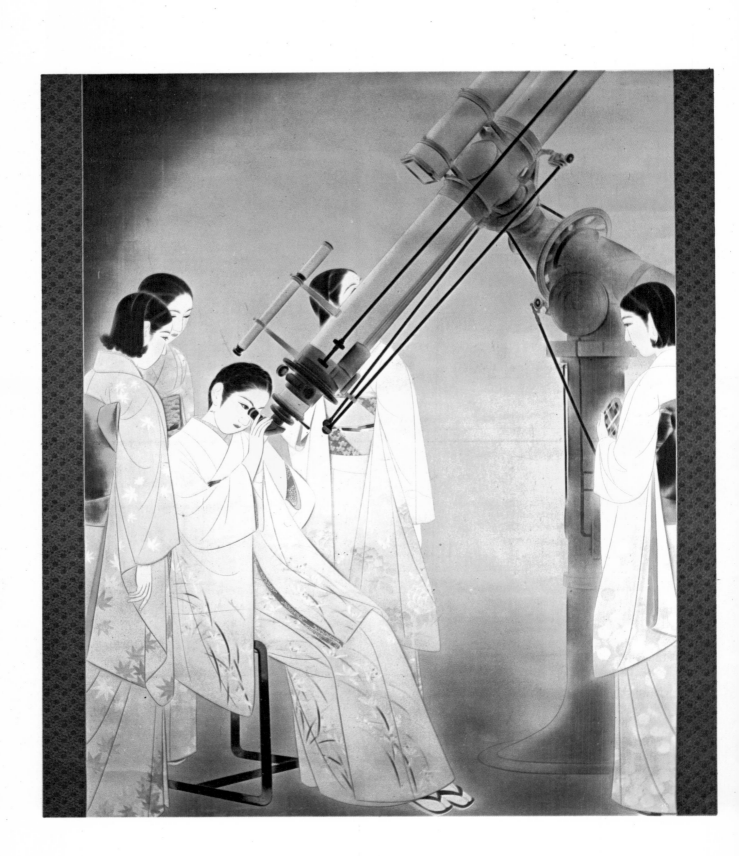

THE WORKS OF ART

291

267 Tomioka raw-silk reeling factory
(jōshū Tomioka seishijō no zu)
(detail); wood block print,
nishiki-e, tryptich; c. 1875
By Ichiyōsai Kuniteru
Tsuneo Tamba Collection, Yokohama

268-269 Fighting Women's Army of Kagoshima (Kagoshima no onna-guntai
rikisen no zu); wood block print,
nishiki-e, tryptich; 1877
By Nagayama Umōsai, published
by Kimura Seisuke
Tsuneo Tamba Collection, Yokohama

268 Instructive stories of self-made
men: portrait of Fukuchi Genichirō
(kyōdo risshi no motoi); wood block
print, nishiki-e; 1885
By Kobayashi Kiyochika, published
by Matsuki Heikichi
Museum of Fine Arts, Boston

270-271 Hara kiri of Saigō Takamori
(Saigō Takamori seppuku zu)
Wood block print, nishiki-e
tryptich; 1877; by Daiso Hōnen
(Yoshitoshi), published by Ōkura
Tsuneo Tamba Collection, Yokohama

272-273 First Industrial Fair in 1877
(tokai meisho no uchi naikoku
kangyō hakuran kai kaijō no zu)
Wood block print, nishiki-e
tryptich; 1877; by Kawanabe Gyōsai
Local History Archives, Ministry
of Education, Tokyo

274-275 Reception for ex-President Grant
at Ueno (Ueno Kōenchi ni oite
Guranto Kun kyōō no zu) (detail)
Wood block print, nishiki-e, 1879
By Yōshū Shūen, published by
Yamamura Kinjirō; Tsuneo Tamba
Collection, Yokohama

276 Ladies with western musical instruments (ōfū fujo sōgaku no zu)
(detail); wood block print,
nishiki-e, tryptich; c. 1890
Published by Ōmori Kakutarō
Museum of Fine Arts, Boston

277 Ladies sewing (kijo saihō no
zu) (detail); wood block print,
nishiki-e, tryptich; 1897
By Shōsai Ginkō, published
by Sasaki; Museum of Fine Arts,
Boston

278-279 First meeting of parliament
(Nihon teikoku kokukai karigi-
jidōzu) (detail); wood block print,
nishiki-e, tryptich; 1890
By Shōsai Ginkō; Local History
Archives, Ministry of Education,
Tokyo

279 Ceremony of the proclamation of
the Imperial constitution (kempō
happu shiki no zu); wood block
print, nishiki-e, tryptich; 1889
By Yōshū Shūen; Tsuneo Tamba
Collection

280 Sergeant Kawasaki crossing the
Taitang River (Kawasaki gunsō
daidōkō wo wataru) (detail)
Wood block print, nishiki-e
tryptich; 1895; published by
Shōgetsudō Matsunaga Sakujirō
Museum of Fine Arts, Boston

280-281 March to attack Weihaiwei (Ikai-
ei kōgeki hyōjō no shingun)
Wood block print, nishiki-e,
tryptich; 1895; by Kobayashi
Kiyochika, published by Shōgetsudō Matsunaga Sakujirō; Tsuneo
Tamba Collection

282 Fighting in the snow (konga sagan
setchū dai-gekisen no kōkei)
Lithograph; 1905; artist unknown
Published as No. 61 of Russo-
Japanese War Memorial Pictures
(Nichi-Ro sensō taishō kinenga)
Hibiya Public Library, Tokyo

283a Battle on the Japan Sea (Nihon-
kai dai kaisen no zu); oil on
canvas; c. 1905; by Tōjō Shōtarō
National Museum of Modern Art
Tokyo

283b Reporting the capture of Port
Arthur (shaka jinei ni oite kami-
tobi wo hishō shite ryojun kanraku
wo teki ni hōzuru no kōkei)
Lithograph; 1905; published as
No. 58 of Russo-Japanese War
Memorial Pictures; Hibiya Public
Library, Tokyo

284 Picture of Ryōunkaku skyscraper
for game (ryōunkaku tōran sugoroku); wood block print, nishiki-e
1890; by Ichijū Kunimasa; Local
History Archives, Ministry of
Education, Tokyo

285 Night scene at Fifth Industrial
Trade Fair, Ueno Park (sangōkan
fukin ō-fujidana no irumineshon)
(detail); lithograph; 1907
By Yamamoto Shōkoku
University of Tokyo

286 Night scene in Yoshiwara (shin
Yoshiwara yo-zakura no kei)
(detail); wood block print, nishiki-e; 1889; by Inoue (?), published by Fukuda Kumajirō
Charles H. Mitchell Collection,
Tokyo

286-287 Funeral procession of Emperor
Meiji (Nijūbashi-gai go-taisō
no zu); wood block print, nishi-
ki-e, two tryptichs; 1912;
By Hampo, published by Mukawa
Unokichi; Tsuneo Tamba Collection

287 Concert using Japanese and Western
instruments (wayō gassō); oil
on canvas; c. 1910; by Sakaki
Teitoku; Takakiyo Mitsui Collection

288 Women watching stars (hoshi wo
miru josei); color on paper; 1936
By Ōta Chōu; National Museum
of Modern Art, Tokyo

Researched and edited in Japanese and English by Madoka Kanai, Shinichi Nagai and Kazuko Yamakawa of Tokyo, and by Miss Ellen Logan of the University of California at Berkeley.

BIBLIOGRAPHY

ASTON, WILLIAM G. tr. *Nihongi (Chronicles Of Japan From The Earliest Times To A.D. 697)*, Japan Society of London, 1896

BEARDSLEY, RICHARD K. and SMITH, ROBERT J. *Japanese Culture; Its Development And Characteristics*, (Tenth Pacific Science Congress), Aldine Publishing Co., 1963

BORTON, HUGH. *Japan's Modern Century*, Ronald Press, 1955

BOXER, CHARLES R. *The Christian Century In Japan*, University of California Press, 1951

BROWN, DELMER. *Nationalism In Japan*. University of California Press, 1955

CHAMBERLAIN, BASIL, tr. *Kojiki (Records Of Ancient Matters)*, Asiatic Society of Japan, 1906

The Complete Journal Of Townsend Harris. Doubleday, 1930

CONNOR, RUSSELL. *Hokusai*, Crown Publishers

EMBREE, JOHN F. *Suye Mura, A Japanese Village*, University of Chicago Press, 1939

GREW, JOSEPH C. *Ten Years In Japan*, Simon and Schuster, 1944

HEARN, LAFCADIO. *Japan, An Attempt At Interpretation*, Grossett and Dunlap, 1904, rev. ed. 1910

IENAGA, SABURŌ. *History Of Japan*, Japan Travel Bureau, 1953, rev. ed. 1962

ISHIMOTO, SHIDZUĒ. *Facing Two Ways*, Farrar and Rinehart, 1935

Japan, The Official Guide, Japan Travel Bureau, 1953, rev. ed. 1962

KAEMMERER, ERIC A. *Trades And Crafts Of Old Japan*, Charles E. Tuttle, 1961

KOMATSU, ISAO. *The Japanese People*, Kokusai Bunka Shinkōkai, Tokyo 1962

MARAINI, FOSCO. *Meeting With Japan*, Hutchinson (London), 1959

MAXON, Y. C. *Control Of Japanese Foreign Policy*, University of California Press, 1957

MICHENER, JAMES. *The Floating World*, Random House, 1954

MUNSTERBERG, HUGO. *The Arts Of Japan, An Illustrated History*, Charles E. Tuttle, 1957

MURASAKI, SHIKIBU. *The Tale Of Genji*, The Literary Guild, 1935

New Japan, Vols. 8-15, Mainichi Newspapers, 1956-63

NORMAN, E. H. *Japan's Emergence As A Modern State*, Institute of Pacific Relations, 1940

OKAKURA, KAKUZŌ. *The Book Of Tea*, Dodd, Mead and Co., 1906

Pageant Of Japanese Art—Painting, Charles E. Tuttle, 1954, rev. ed. 1957

Pageant Of Japanese Art—Sculpture, Charles E. Tuttle, 1953, rev. ed. 1958

REISCHAUER, EDWIN O. *Japan Past And Present*, Alfred A. Knopf, 1953

REISCHAUER, ROBERT K. *Japan, Government And Politics*, Nelson, 1939

SANSOM, GEORGE B. *A History Of Japan To 1334*, Stanford University Press, 1958

SANSOM, GEORGE B. *A History Of Japan 1334-1615*, Stanford University Press, 1961

SANSOM, GEORGE B. *A History Of Japan 1615-1867*, Stanford University Press, 1963

SANSOM, GEORGE B. *Japan, A Short Cultural History*, D. Appleton-Century, 1931, rev. ed. 1962

SANSOM, GEORGE B. *The Western World And Japan*, Alfred A. Knopf, 1950

Sources Of Japanese Tradition, compiled by Ryūsaku Tsunoda, William Theodore de Bary, Donald Keene, Columbia University Press, 1960

STATLER, OLIVER. *Japanese Inn*, Random House, 1961

STORRY, RICHARD. *A History Of Modern Japan*, Penguin Books, 1960, rev. ed. 1963

SUZUKI, DAISETZ TEITARŌ. *Studies In Zen*, Philosophical Library, 1955

This Is Japan, Vols. 4-10, Asahi Shimbun, 1957-63

Travels Of Marco Polo, edited by Manuel Komroff, Boni and Liveright, 1930

WALWORTH, ARTHUR. *Black Ships Off Japan*, Alfred Knopf, 1941

YANAGA, CHITOSHI. *Japan Since Perry*, McGraw-Hill, 1949

[CONTINUED FROM FRONT FLAP]

commissioned by a thirteenth-century warrior to commemorate his exploits in battle) to the face of the Meiji Emperor daringly portrayed on a Nishiki-e print, the book follows the course of Japanese history and the developing styles and techniques of Japanese art.

Japan—A History in Art is divided into ten historical periods, from the Archaic to the Meiji, each preceded by a detailed historical and art chronology. The appendix contains complete data on every work of art reproduced. The photography was made possible through the cooperation of Japan's principal curators and private collectors. In selecting the art works and preparing the narrative, the author had the opportunity of consulting with leading scholars in Japan and the West.

The matchless collection of pictures superbly photographed, the lively and authoritative text, the magnificent printing and binding by Toppan of Tokyo—every page is in full color—combine to make what is perhaps the most remarkable and beautiful story of a people and its culture ever published.